Praise for *Tell Me a Story*

Scott is a genius! This book is inspiring, challenging, and a lighthouse that calls us to a new narrative. I loved this book and you will too!

Jon Acuff
WALL STREET JOURNAL BESTSELLING AUTHOR OF *QUITTER* AND *STUFF CHRISTIANS LIKE*

One of the great tragedies of our time is that the Christian community is losing its story. In today's distracted and disrupted culture, the church's voice is fading, because we've lost sight of the power of story. Scott McClellan's fascinating new book *Tell Me a Story* is a timely reminder that to engage a media-driven world effectively, we need to get back to the mindset of Jesus—telling compelling stories that transform lives.

Phil Cooke, PhD
FILMMAKER, MEDIA CONSULTANT, AUTHOR OF *UNIQUE: TELLING YOUR STORY IN THE AGE OF BRANDS AND SOCIAL MEDIA*

Tell Me a Story is an invitation to embrace the story of God unfolding in all of our lives. It's a witty, insightful, and practical look into the raw beauty of story and its transformative power.

Charles Lee
CEO OF IDEATION, AUTHOR OF *GOOD IDEA. NOW WHAT?*

Tell Me a Story is a reminder that the life of following Jesus is not a rigid, legalistic experience, but a story in which we get to breathe and live. Through these pages, Scott writes of God's invitation for all of us to surrender our character, conflict, narrative, purpose, and plot to God, the greatest storyteller of all time.

Amena Brown
AUTHOR AND SPOKEN WORD POET

In *Tell Me a Story*, Scott McClellan offers the next generation of leaders a fresh, personal, and inspiring way of seeing themselves and their place in the world. Scott calls each of us to be storytellers, and it's a call I hope we answer.

Brad Lomenick,
PRESIDENT AND LEAD VISIONARY OF CATALYST

I have long believed in the incredible power of story. Scott reignited that belief and will make you believe it too.

Blaine Hogan
AUTHOR OF *UNTITLED: THOUGHTS ON THE CREATIVE PROCESS*

I opened this book and found myself "right in the middle of a page-turner." Scott has a compelling way of sharing his story and the stories of others while leaving room for mine. You want to know how he does it? Get this book. Not only will you get the answer to that question, you'll also find out what gobsmacked, group freak out, and hip-dislocating mojo has to do with anything.

Kem Meyer
COMMUNICATIONS DIRECTOR AT GRANGER COMMUNITY CHURCH,
AUTHOR OF *LESS CLUTTER. LESS NOISE.*

Scott McClellan is a gifted writer who crafts each and every word into beautiful sentences, compelling the reader into the narrative journey of their lives. And *Tell Me a Story* did just that. It continually drew me into the belief that my story mattered, and that God wants to use it. And as I began to believe that my story mattered, I began to not only encounter, but pay more attention to the daily work of God in my life.

This is the type of book I want to hand to people in my pastoral and counseling work and say, "Your story matters . . . you need to share it with others." But it's not just a book for others; it is a book for me. It's a book that reminds me that because my story matters to God, I'm to come alongside others and encourage them to live out and tell their story.

Rhett Smith
MARRIAGE AND FAMILY THERAPIST, AUTHOR OF *THE ANXIOUS CHRISTIAN*

Tell Me a Story is a book that needs to be read, written by an author who needs to write it. Scott McClellan has combined his spiritual depth with his dry humor, and has given the world this timely and beautiful work of art. The more we visit and revisit the story we're caught in, the more we'll find ourselves living out our highest calling of Christ in us, through us, and in spite of us. I thank God for Scott's voice—a voice that calls us back into both the telling, and into the living out, of the only Story that really matters.

Gary A. Molander
OWNER AND FOUNDER OF FLOODGATE PRODUCTIONS,
AUTHOR OF *PURSUING CHRIST. CREATING ART.*

Few people are as capable as Scott McClellan to write a book like this. In recent years, he has become one of the most trusted Christian voices on effective communication. In *Tell Me a Story*, Scott seeks to empower readers to become captivating and compelling storytellers. You'd do well to listen to what he has to say.

Jonathan Merritt
FAITH AND CULTURE WRITER,
AUTHOR OF *A FAITH OF OUR OWN: FOLLOWING JESUS BEYOND THE CULTURE WARS*

tell
me
a
story

tell me a story

Finding God *(and Ourselves)* Through Narrative

SCOTT McCLELLAN

MOODY PUBLISHERS
CHICAGO

All Scripture quotations, unless otherwise indicated, are taken from the *Holy Bible, New International Version®*, NIV®. Copyright ©1973, 1978, 1984, 2011 by Biblica, Inc.™ Used by permission of Zondervan. All rights reserved worldwide. www.zondervan.com

Scripture quotations marked MSG are from *The Message*, copyright © by Eugene H. Peterson 1993, 1994, 1995. Used by permission of NavPress Publishing Group.

Edited by Pam Pugh
Interior Design: Design Corps
Cover Design: Faceout Studio
Cover Image: Shutterstock / 93315331

Library of Congress Cataloging-in-Publication Data

McClellan, Scott.
  Tell me a story : finding God (and ourselves) through narrative / Scott McClellan.
       p. cm.
  Includes bibliographical references.
  ISBN 978-0-8024-0856-3
  1. Storytelling—Religious aspects—Christianity. I. Title.
  BT83.78.M375 2013
  248.4'6—dc23

                              2012038363

We hope you enjoy this book from Moody Publishers. Our goal is to provide high-quality, thought-provoking books and products that connect truth to your real needs and challenges. For more information on other books and products written and produced from a biblical perspective, go to www.moodypublishers.com or write to:

Moody Publishers
820 N. LaSalle Boulevard
Chicago, IL 60610

1 3 5 7 9 10 8 6 4 2

To my girls, Elise and Maggie,
who have taught me far more than I've taught them.
And to my wife, Annie,
who makes every story better through her kindness and strength.

contents

foreword

WHEN I WAS YOUNG, MY dad used to tell me stories before bed. These were tales that rivaled those of Tom Sawyer or Huck Finn—only they were true. He told me about growing up in Chicago, the same place where I was born, but our experiences were vastly different.

Each night, I got to hear a different story from my dad. He told me about the time he saw a UFO or when Santa Claus broke into his bedroom to give him a candy cane. I became the audience of a master storyteller, enthralled with the unusual and interesting characters from another lifetime. These were incredible, audacious tales of bravery and adventure. And I was immediately captivated.

Every night, I would go to bed amazed. And every night, my dad would tell me the same thing: "Some day, you'll have stories of your own to tell." But I never believed him. There was just no way I'd ever have stories like my dad's—I was certain of it. They were just too incredible. And for the longest time, I was right.

FINDING MY STORY

For many years, I lived an average life of safety and security. I got good grades, didn't get into trouble, and never broke a bone. I lived a boring story. I knew this; I just didn't know how to fix it.

Not until I left home for college did I find a deeper narrative into which I could immerse myself. I began to travel and slowly started coming alive. At first, the trips were small—weekend jaunts with friends and such. Then they evolved into entire summers, road-tripping across the country to work for the summer. Eventually, my wanderlust led me out of the country on a study abroad program in Spain, which was where I started grasping what it meant to live a truly great story.

On the streets of Seville, I met a homeless man named Micah. As a kid who grew up in a farm town, I never spent much time around homelessness, so meeting someone who lived on the streets was uncomfortable. I didn't have a neat and tidy compartment in which to place such an experience. So I did what most people would do: I walked away.

I ignored the man, at first pretending I didn't see him and then downright dismissing him. My friends and I had plans for the evening; we were going to check out the city's nightlife. We didn't have time for vagrants. We told Micah we'd come back later (we were lying).

"Will you be here tomorrow?" my friend asked.

Micah shook his head: "I could be here, there, I could be anywhere—I could be DEAD tomorrow."

The statement shocked me, but I wasn't affected enough to actually do anything. So I walked away. As I did, Micah started screaming at us, begging for help. My pace quickened, and Micah's shouts got quieter in my ears, all the while growing louder in my mind.

The faster and farther I went, the more I could hear his voice. It was unbearable.

Finally, I stopped. Handing my backpack to my roommate, I told him there was something I had to take care of. And I did what I didn't want to do: I turned around. I'm not sure why; I just knew I needed to. And what happened next changed my life.

I treated Micah to a McDonald's hamburger meal. As he stuffed his face with fries and drenched the partially chewed food with his drink, I tried to talk to start a conversation. At first, he just listened, but then he spoke up, asking me why I came back. I told him I had to. That I couldn't really explain it, but just knew I needed to turn around. Then he told me something that I'll never forget:

"You are the only one."

"What do you mean?" I asked.

"I've been standing on that street corner for months, and you are the only one who stopped."

I couldn't believe what he was saying. I refused to accept it. However, he insisted it was true.

After about an hour, Micah and I shook hands and parted ways. I never saw him again. But I was never able to look at a homeless person—much less anyone in need—the same way again.

INCITING INCIDENTS

Sometimes, that's all it takes to change a story. A simple change of mind. One act that alters the course of your life forever. Turning around when you'd rather run away.

Think of the stories you grew up with. *Star Wars. Lord of the Rings. Catcher in the Rye. Casablanca. The Matrix.* In each and every epic that moves us, there is an element of surprise, some unexpected turn that sends the hero on a journey. Storytelling experts call this the "inciting incident." It's the event that calls a character, often unwillingly, into a larger story. And it is always uncomfortable.

The word "incite" means to stir into action, and that's what all great stories do. They change us in some way, make us move. This book does just that. It's not only a picture of what it takes to live a significant story. It's also a framework for how we tell that story to others—and invite them to join us.

My friend Scott has given us a look into the story of our lives and the larger story in which we all can choose to participate.

What's more, he's demonstrated that it's not enough to believe in a good story; you also have to live one.

Whether we realize it or not, we all are storytellers. With the lives we are living and the risks we are, or aren't, taking, we are crafting a narrative for eternity. For those who would dare to live differently, the road before us is not the path of least resistance. It's scary and costly, full of unexpected twists and turns. But on this jagged journey, we find the one thing we're searching for: meaning.

ANSWERING THE QUESTION

For years, I never understood why I didn't have stories like my dad. But now I do. There was one difference between my childhood and his: risk. It wasn't until I encountered this truth—that without conflict a story is incomplete—did my life change.

All our favorite films and books are telling us the same thing: Safety is not what you were made for. Most of us want our lives to matter, but few are living differently. Why is this? Because we're afraid of the cost (I know I am). We know that it's only in the throes of danger that men and women become heroes. And this scares us (as it should).

But we must consider the cost of not risking safety and comfort. Where would Middle Earth be if Bilbo Baggins had never left the Shire? What would have become of a galaxy far, far away if Luke Skywalker stayed on the farm? In our own lives, there is a similar question. This book will help you answer it.

Jeff Goins
AUTHOR OF *WRECKED*. GOINSWRITER.COM

things fall apart

WE WERE A YEAR INTO our adoption process when the wheels started to come off. International relations between the United States and Vietnam were breaking down, and it appeared the two countries might not renew their intercountry adoption agreement when it would expire six months later. What was supposed to simply be a long process suddenly became an at-risk process.

NOT A MATCH

In February 2008, in order to proceed with the adoption journey we were convinced God had prompted us to start, Annie and I had to sign a waiver. In it we acknowledged that we might not be matched to a child before the current agreement expired, that a new agreement might not be reached, and that we might lose all the time and money we'd invested in our adoption.

We also had to acknowledge that we might be crushed if things didn't work out, although that part wasn't explicitly stated in the waiver.

We stepped out in faith, signed the waiver, and then the bad news started. Some families couldn't get visas for their kids and they were stuck in Vietnam. A flu outbreak in a large orphanage rendered many previously eligible children ineligible for international adoption. The days on the calendar began to run out as we twisted in the wind, so desperate for good news, so desperate to become parents.

In July we got the call from our caseworker. "Three children are going to be matched to families, but you're number four on the list," she said. "I'm sorry, we don't have a baby for you." The risk waiver we'd signed months earlier now read like a prophecy, and we were crushed just as we had acknowledged we might be. As Annie wrote at the time, it's difficult to let go of a dream you've nurtured for two years.

By the time all of this happened, I'd been a Christian for more than a decade, and quite frankly, I didn't expect to have a crisis of faith. But that's what happened. After all, adopting a child wasn't even our idea—it was God's idea. We'd been so sure when we sensed Him leading us to start our family this way that we simply responded. (If we're being honest, I took my sweet time coming around to the idea. At one point I was tempted to flee like Jonah fled from God's call to go to Nineveh.) How could God's idea go so terribly wrong? How could something that started out so good become so painful?

I confess that I assumed God wasn't in it anymore, either because we'd done something wrong or because He simply moved on to someone or something more interesting. (Yes, I occasionally make God in my own image, and yes, I'm aware that's a problem.) This conclusion, paired with our grief, led to some dark days. I still believed in God, but my circumstances caused me to wonder how He felt about me. Thankfully, God used two things to rescue us from our despair, and in a way, both of them were story.

A FRAME FOR OUR PAIN

A few months into our adoption journey, Annie and I started a blog. I wish we could say we had grand or benevolent intentions, but really we were tired. Tired of answering the same questions over and over again. Tired of being asked, "Any news on the adoption front?" and having to say, "Nope. No news. None whatsoever," over and over again. So we started a blog. We answered several frequently asked questions, shared where we were in the process, and outlined what was next.

As you might imagine, the tone of our blog changed after we signed that waiver. At times we were scared. At times we were impatient. At times we were frustrated with the whole thing. But we were still hopeful, and we kept returning to the assurance that we'd felt led to start this journey.

What we didn't realize was that while we were telling our story, we were inviting our friends and family into it. Our little ad hoc community shared in our optimism and anxiety, so when we received that terrible phone call from our caseworker, we didn't grieve alone. That support was the first thing God used to rescue us, and it meant the world to us.

> Conflict isn't what ruins a story—far from it! Conflict is what makes a story great.

The second thing God gave us was a frame for our pain. It was August 2008 and Annie and I were at the first Echo Conference. I wasn't very involved with the conference back then, but I was pitching in where I could while the rest of my colleagues at RT Creative Group did all the hard work. The second night of the conference, we took our seats in anticipation of hearing Donald Miller, because we enjoyed his books. As he spoke that night about how story structure might help us lead better lives, I struggled to keep up. The concept seemed so foreign to me. But when he got to the part about conflict—an essential element of any good story—it was as though he was talking directly to us, offering us a new way to look at what we'd endured the past few months.

Yes, there is conflict, Miller seemed to say, *and yes, God loves you.* Seen through the frame of story, those two ideas were no longer at odds with each other in my mind. Miller explained that conflict isn't what ruins a story—far from it! Conflict is what makes a story great. If that idea is as foreign to you now as it was to me then, take a moment and try to think of a great story in which the protagonist wasn't put through the ringer. No such story exists.

Miller said that while we sometimes advertise Jesus as a product that will fix all our problems and spare us from conflict, the Bible declares the opposite to be true. He also said that while we sometimes encounter conflict, shrug our shoulders, and say, "Oh well, I guess God closed that door," some things are worth pursuing no matter what. Even if you have to kick down a few doors.

Hurting as I was, I was gobsmacked. Our story wasn't over, not by a long shot. We were right in the middle of a page-turner. More important, God was right in the middle of it, too.

COMMUNAL STORY

Soon we were ready to press on. We'd been called to adoption and it was time to get on with it. If Vietnam wasn't going to work, and if we couldn't kick that door down without sparking an international incident, we'd pick another country. Wherever we landed, we were convinced that the end of this story would go something like, "you and me and baby makes three." We were doing okay. In fact, it was right as we were getting our paperwork and money sorted out so that we could transfer to our agency's Ethiopia program that we got another call from our caseworker.

"You're not going to believe this, but we think we have a baby for you."

She was right; we didn't believe her. We were days—*days*— away from Vietnam closing to US adoptions (more than three years later, the process hasn't reopened) and this new plot twist seemed too good to be true. There was a baby girl and she might be ours. They sent us pictures and we fawned over her big brown eyes.

This was another risk—we could become emotionally attached to a little face we might never meet.

As it turned out, nothing was guaranteed yet. There was still one more hurdle we had to clear before the deadline, but we would know one way or the other by the end of the week. Over the course of the week, our hopes hinged on paperwork and approval that normally took three weeks to secure. We, along with many from our little community, prayed like madmen and madwomen those five days. Friday was it—make or break. This was a communal story that changed each of its participants in one way or another.

The call came. We heard the words we'd been waiting so long to hear. We would be parents. *Her* parents. There was crying and laughing and jumping and hugging and *Thank You God Thank You God Thank You.* And it didn't all come from Annie and me. Like I said before about our little community, they didn't let us grieve alone when we were at our lowest. Well, they didn't let us celebrate alone either. It was a group freak-out. Our Facebook, Twitter, and email accounts exploded with joy and congratulations, which we saved and later incorporated into our daughter's life book so she would know that part of her story.

Somehow, this little baby, this story, belonged to all of us. These people traveled with us, hoped with us, waited with us, and ached with us. They prayed and pleaded along with us. This was a collective victory, a communal story that changed each of its participants in one way or another. I know it changed me.

For one thing, I'm a dad. This seems like a miracle in itself. But I'm also a believer in the power of story to change the world. Lauren Winner uses an interesting phrase, "theology for the middle,"[1] which reminds me of what I'm getting at here. Meaning I don't know exactly how or when all of this got started, nor how or when it will end. There was creation, the fall, Abraham, David, and the prophets. Then there was the incarnation, the crucifixion, the resurrection, and the ascension. All of this happened—it has been done. Looking ahead, there will be the second coming and the re-creation of all things.

All of this will happen—it will be done.

YOU . . . A STORYTELLER

In the meantime, in between, in the middle, here we are. Now, how should we play this thing out? What does God want us to do while we're here? We know we're not responsible for what He has already done or what He has said He will do, and yet He has plans in mind for us. To the extent we can find and articulate what it means to follow and serve God in between His grand tent poles of human history, what we're doing is sketching out a theology for the middle. I'm of the opinion, if you're wondering, that story is a helpful construct for developing a theology for the middle because it gives us a sense of who God is, who we are, and how we ought to spend the allowances we've been given.

I don't have life or story or God figured out, nor do I know the particulars of how my life will play out. As such, this isn't my book of answers or my road map to a smarter, taller, richer you. This book is my attempt to convince you that seeing everything through the lens of story will help you make some sense of life and faith and yourself. The ideas, thoughts, and truths I've strung together here represent the book I wish someone had given me when I was agonizing over where to go to college, when I felt so lost after graduating, or when I couldn't find meaning in the broken pieces of our adoption process.

Story is who we are, where we've been, and where we're going. Story is a call to action. Story is an invitation into something bigger than ourselves. Story is the belief that the darkest hour is just before dawn. Story is the conviction that conflict does not mean chaos.

Story is the structure through which God gives us His gospel and sends us out into the world. Story is a lens through which we might see the world and better understand its meaning and movements.

Story changes everything. My hope and prayer is that this book will convince you to identify yourself as a storyteller, an artist committed to narrative, and that in so doing you'll experience God and your life more deeply than you did before.

story:
a new way to see

*"Story changes everything. Identify yourself as a storyteller,
an artist committed to narrative, and you'll experience
God and your life more deeply than you did before."*

THE IDEA OF THIS BOOK is that story is a great tool for helping us understand life and faith. But when we read parts of the Bible that aren't narratives, such as the New Testament epistles, the story lens still proves meaningful. Peter and Paul were real people with stories, writing letters to real people they loved, urging them to live better stories. Knowing these men's biographies helps us better appreciate the weight and integrity of their words.

REAL PEOPLE

It may sound like good advice when Peter writes, "Cast all your anxiety on him because he cares for you."[1] But when we consider the man who composed those words, we know it's more than a platitude waiting to be cross-stitched on a decorative pillow. We know he made his share of mistakes as a disciple of Christ, and we know he denied knowing Jesus three times following Judas's betrayal. We know Peter was gently restored to service by the risen Christ, and we know he preached boldly on the day of Pentecost. We know his leadership was vital to the early church, and credible tradition tells us Peter died for his faith at the hands of Nero's goons.

When that man, with that story, tells me to give my anxiety to the God who cares for me, I'm listening.

Knowing Paul's story from Acts and the places in his letters where he offered up bits of his biography, we know the man went through a lot (e.g., 2 Corinthians 11:24–27). When he wrote, "We are hard pressed on every side, but not crushed; perplexed, but not in despair; persecuted, but not abandoned; struck down, but not destroyed" (2 Corinthians 4:8–9), we know he wasn't indulging in hyperbole. Thus when Paul teaches about love (1 Corinthians 13), perseverance (Romans 5:4), and the surpassing joy of knowing Christ (Philippians 3:8), his story undergirds his words. Even in the epistles we find a story at work—real people writing to real people, guiding them in their pursuit of a real God.

THE SCHEMER'S LIMP

There's a man in the Bible named Jacob—do you know who I'm talking about? Jacob is the one who covered his smooth hands with goatskins in order to deceive his blind, elderly father, Isaac, into believing he was his exceptionally swarthy brother, Esau. No, really, read it for yourself in Genesis 27. Jacob tricked his father into giving him the blessing as the firstborn, leaving Esau with the short end of the paternal blessing stick.

A few chapters later, in Genesis 32, Jacob is afraid for his life. Esau isn't just hairy, he's murderously angry and determined to get revenge on Jacob. At this point, Jacob knows a showdown with Esau is inevitable, and he doesn't appear to like his chances. Instead, he sends out livestock and messengers in hopes of appeasing Esau and negotiating some sort of truce.

It's in the midst of all this that Jacob finds himself alone one night, having divided up all his assets and sent them away. Suddenly, Jacob finds himself wrestling an unknown opponent until dawn. I'll let *The Message* take it from here:

> When the man saw that he couldn't get the best of Jacob as they wrestled, he deliberately threw Jacob's hip out of joint.
>
> The man said, "Let me go; it's daybreak."
>
> Jacob said, "I'm not letting you go 'til you bless me."
>
> The man said, "What's your name?"
>
> He answered, "Jacob."
>
> The man said, "But no longer. Your name is no longer Jacob. From now on it's Israel (God-Wrestler); you've wrestled with God and you've come through."
>
> Jacob asked, "And what's your name?"
>
> The man said, "Why do you want to know my name?" And then, right then and there, he blessed him.
>
> Jacob named the place Peniel (God's Face) because, he said, "I saw God face-to-face and lived to tell the story!"
>
> The sun came up as he left Peniel, limping because of his hip.[2]

I don't fully understand what this story means, and I'm not sure Jacob did either, but I fully understand that it's meaningful. Jacob was a schemer—first he'd duped his brother Esau out of his birthright for a pot of soup, and then duped Isaac out of Esau's blessing. Jacob was on the run, desperate and doing what he could to assuage Esau's wrath.

Then, apropos of nothing, this mysterious midnight wrestler appears. Their struggle concludes with some hip-dislocating mojo, and Jacob leaves a changed man. For one thing, he has a limp (rarely a sign of honor). For another thing, he has a new name: Israel. And finally, he has a new attitude. When he and Esau meet again, Israel the Limper (formerly Jacob the Schemer) is determined to *give* to his brother rather than *take* from him. "God has been good to me," Israel insists, "and I have more than enough."[3]

I don't tell you this story so that you'll be persuaded to wreak havoc in your family, wrestle a stranger, and limp your way into reconciliation. This is not, as near as I can tell, an ordained formula for bettering the human experience. I tell you this story because God chose to tell us this story. I tell you this story because it's a good story. This is a story in which a flawed human being is confronted with the consequences of his choices, is confronted with the reality of God, and is somehow redeemed through an encounter that seems, if you don't mind my saying, utterly fantastical.

In this story I see conflict, mystery, redemption, hope, and transformation. I see God's presence in the strife and striving of His people. I see an acknowledgment of the value of story in Jacob's commemoration of the narrative. Remember, he gave the place a name that meant "God's Face" because, he said, "I saw God face-to-face and lived to tell the story!" He lived to tell the story, and tell the story is exactly what he did.

THE "MANUAL"? OR THE "STORY"?

Even if you go to church every Sunday, it may have been awhile since you heard a preacher or teacher tell a good story. For many of us, exploring the Bible and pursuing spiritual growth are increasingly driven by the practice of extracting and identifying principles for better living. Sometimes these principles even start with the same letter (e.g., Faith, Family, Fellowship, and Follow-Up). But for all their good intentions, these principles rarely compel the kind of life change they promise. We return the next week, hungry once again, hoping the principles will stick to our ribs this time. The truth is that it doesn't have to be this way. Jesus didn't call us to a Principle Driven Life, but rather to His gospel, the Good News, a story that ushers in a kingdom.

I've often wondered how many people, if we snuck truth serum into their morning coffee, would admit to being annoyed by all the narrative in the Bible. Particularly the Old Testament, which kicks off with "In the beginning" and doesn't take a break from story until Leviticus begins ninety chapters later. I wonder if when we read these stories we're conditioned to leapfrog from one doctrine or principle to another: "Seven-day creation . . . skip ahead . . . original sin . . . skip ahead . . . Abrahamic covenant . . . skip ahead . . ." and so on.

Perhaps this is because we enjoy the comfort and convenience of a Christianity that squares nicely with PowerPoint templates. And yet the Bible, in its raw and undomesticated state, doesn't look anything like a slide deck full of bullet points and bar graphs, does it? Ironically, we who espouse a "high view of Scripture" often seem dead set on making the Bible what we want it to be.

A former Sunday school teacher of mine, a man for whom I have the utmost respect, carried a Bible on which he'd had the words "The Manual" embossed on the spine. I suppose this makes some sense because the Bible contains indispensable insights and applications for life. Also, this man spent the first half of his professional life as an engineer of some sort, so he

> If I had to get a new label embossed on the spine of my Bible, I think I'd choose "The Story."

was likely predisposed to see the world in terms of complicated processes and machinery that required the ultimate manual. But does "The Manual" really fit?

I don't know that Isaiah, Daniel, Job, or Jonah would apply that label to the books that bear their names. Some of the psalms are instructive, but even their form is often more artful than informational. While we find books that are predominantly instructive, such as Proverbs or James, they're hardly as exhaustive as we'd expect from a proper manual. Neither are they structured to guide us step-by-step through life, but you get the point.

I've spent more than a decade thinking about "The Manual" and attempting to articulate my unease with it. As labels go, I think I prefer some variation of the standard *Holy Bible* or "the Word of God." But if I had to get a new label embossed on the spine of my Bible (yes, I realize this is an odd hypothetical), something I believed more accurately conveyed the contents of the book, I think I'd choose "The Story."

A CHARACTER WHO WANTS SOMETHING

Before we go any further, we should probably define our terms. Robert McKee is the authority on American screenwriting and the author of *Story,* his guide to the craft of storytelling. Although *Story* is more than four hundred pages long, McKee doesn't dwell on a definition of story—he moves from a brief romantic philosophy of storytelling into an exhaustive, methodical exposition of its elements. But early on he does offer us this:

"A story is simply one huge master event," he writes. "When you look at the value-charged situation in the life of the character at the beginning of the story, then compare it to the value-charge at the end of the story, you should see the *arc of the film,* the great sweep of change that takes life from one condition at the opening to a changed condition at the end. This final condition, the end change, must be *absolute* and *irreversible*."[4]

In *A Million Miles in a Thousand Years,* Donald Miller recounts the experience of attending McKee's Story seminar with his friend Jordan. After thirty-six hours of lecture and pages upon pages of notes, it was Jordan who finally offered an accessible definition of story: "A story is a character who wants something and overcomes conflict to get it."[5] That's a definition we can get our arms around, and as Miller explores to great effect in his book, it's a definition we can observe at work in compelling stories and lives.

In terms of simplicity, Kurt Vonnegut's description of classic story structure—"Man in Hole"—can't be beat. As you might imagine, this means a story is what happens when a man falls in a hole, and then tries to climb out. Of course, "the story needn't be about a man or a hole," Vonnegut said.[6] Rather, the hole could be grief, injury, unrequited love, or a city bus rigged to explode if the speedometer dips below 55 miles per hour.

In any of these definitions or classifications, story is about pursuit. Story is movement by a character or group of characters from one point (physical, emotional, or otherwise) to another point. A story is progress, action toward an outcome. Characters without this pursuit do not make for a story. A conversation is not a story. A movie about characters who don't progress toward anything would be the equivalent of security footage from an uneventful day inside a shopping mall. "Objective is the driving force of fiction," writes

> "A story is a character who wants something and overcomes conflict to get it."

James Scott Bell. "It generates forward motion and keeps the Lead from just sitting around."[7]

Let's go back to my story, the one I told you in the introduction. Annie and I are the lead characters, although of the two of us only she looks like a movie star (I look like a young Hogwarts professor). We had an objective—to adopt a child. Enter stage right: Conflict. In our case, conflict didn't mean life or death, but it did present us with a choice to make. We could cut our emotional and financial losses and move on. We could say we misunderstood God, we'd simply made a mistake. Or we could continue our pursuit toward the objective.

As humans, we often tend toward the path of least resistance. We skip the stairs and take the elevator. We skip the book and read the CliffsNotes. We use the entrance with the automatic sliding doors. And most important, we don't put our emotions and savings on the line and take on the Vietnamese government when there's an easier way. Well, we don't do any of these things *unless we have an objective,* unless we're pursuing something that's worth the hardship.

When we become people who want something that's worth overcoming resistance, we no longer settle for the default Path of Least Resistance mode. That's the beginning of the power of story—to propel us toward *something*—but it gets better. Story is so much bigger than just what we want. Story helps us see beyond ourselves to the forward momentum of our Father's world, His kingdom, and our place in it.

IT KEEPS ON HAPPENING AND IS HAPPENING STILL

In response to all of this talk about story, some might say, "Jesus died for me, and that's all I need to know." Okay, then. I'd say this response at least hints at a story, doesn't it? And yet it's been gutted, reduced to a proposition that's hardly compelling to those of us who already believe it, let alone anyone who doesn't. A proposition like this practically begs for the rest of the story, particularly if we're halfway curious.

Jesus died for me.

Wait, who died?

Jesus, God's Son.

Okay, but why did He die for you?

Well, uh, let me back up a little bit . . .

This is what I'm saying. The story is so much better. It's the introduction to both God and humanity in the garden; it's the infection of sin and the beginning of a legacy of separation; it's the twists and turns of a reclamation project that spans continents and centuries; it's the living and active God who gives us life, movement, and being in Himself; it's the hopeful pilgrimage toward the Holy City.

Yes, the gospel is a narrative, not a truism. Frederick Buechner called it a fairy tale with "one crucial difference from all other fairy tales, which is that the claim made for it is that it is true, that it not only happened once upon a time but has kept on happening ever since and is happening still."[8]

I'll say it again—the story (of which God is the Author) is so much better.

THE RIGHT STORIES

I guess you could say that I'm "pro-story," if you're into those kinds of red state/blue state distinctions. The fact is I'm about to spend dozens of pages and thousands of words advocating that you become pro-story too, but it's important that we recognize that all stories are not created equal. What I mean is that not all compelling stories are virtuous, and not all virtuous stories are compelling. Not all stories are redemptive, not all stories are honest. Not all stories are hopeful. Some stories are harmful, some exploitative. Some stories are birthed from good intentions but miss the mark.

Henri Nouwen wrote, "Many people in this life suffer because they are anxiously searching for the man or woman, the event or encounter, which will take their loneliness away,"[9] and so it's important to note that story is not God. Story is not a saving ideology. Story won't fix you in and of itself. Story is not alive—it didn't make you and it can't save you. What I'm presenting in this book is the idea that story is a mechanism, a process for discovery, a compass of sorts, and a framework for understanding.

Every religion and cult and philosophy and separatist militia has a story. Every politician, marketer, defense attorney, and con man has a story. The worst books, movies, musicals, plays, and television shows ever written all have a story. The wrong stories—

> Story is not just where we are, it's where we came from and where we're going.

or even the right stories in the wrong hands—can be used to distract, mislead, divide, abuse, and enslave. So while I'm pro-story, it's never enough to simply have a story. The message that *story and storytellers matter* is not the same as *any story will do.*

The fact that stories can and do go wrong should strengthen our resolve, not undermine it. The abuse of story does not poison the form. Our work, then, is to find, follow, and tell the right stories. This is the shape of the life for which we were made.

When we become storytellers, narrative people, we start to change. It starts with how we organize information and events. Then our ears start to perk up when we hear others tell their stories. Eventually, we see the narrative in everything and we see everything through the narrative. Story is not just outcome, it's the process that precedes and follows every outcome. Story is not just what we have, it's how we got what we have and what we're going to do with it. Story is not just where we are, it's where we came from and where we're going.

Seeing the narrative in all things means taking a long view. What I mean by that is if you want to truly tell the story of World War II, you're going to need to back up a few decades to the end of World War I—any history buff will tell you that. Choices have precursors and consequences. Conflict has context. Circumstances and trials can be redeemed because of their positive effects on us. Short-term thinking and shortcuts aren't good enough. Neither are casual propositions and truisms.

It's good to have principles to live by, but it's better to practice those principles while we're on a journey. I'm all for morality, but morality in isolation lacks meaning. Morality paired with mission, what we might call "morality on the way," provides a foundation for our character as we make choices—it helps us stay the course when we face conflict, resistance, and indecision.

THE WHOLE TRUTH

Through the frame of the right story, the past is marked by grace and the future teems with hope. In the present, we acknowledge both and commit ourselves to the pursuit. So what do the right stories look like? I like the way Donald Miller once described *Blue Like Jazz: The Movie*—"It's a story that tells the truth."[10]

The right stories tell the truth. And just as important, the right stories don't settle for partial truth. "I failed," may be a true story, but it's not the whole story because it makes no mention of redemption through forgiveness or perseverance. As long as we tell ourselves a story like that, the wrong story, we're deceiving ourselves with a grain of truth. If we want the whole truth, something that's faithful to the world we really live in, we need a story that refuses to end with, "I failed." The truth is our failures are not the end of us, and the right stories tell this truth. The whole truth.

In William Shakespeare's *Henry IV*, Hotspur declares, "O while you live, tell truth and shame the devil!"[11] Amen, Brother Hotspur. True stories shame the devil to the extent that they tell the whole truth—good, bad, ugly, and divine. True stories shame the devil to the extent that their point of view is personal but not myopic. True stories lend perspective to that which we've chosen to pursue *(Is this really worth it?)* and the conflict that invariably befalls us *(Is this really the end of the world?)*.

Early in his gospel John describes Jesus by saying, "In him was life, and that life was the light of all mankind" (1:4). This light—by which we see life as it really is—properly orients us to the truth. Jesus arrived telling a story about who He was and what He intended to do in and through people. The story shed light on the heart of God, the plight of humanity, and what happens when the two are brought together by grace. Jesus had a story to tell, and as we'll talk about more later, He commissioned His followers to bear that story.

If we dare answer such a call and go tumbling down the rabbit hole, we're given new eyes with which to see the truth in story. If you're willing, let's go on by using these new eyes to look into a mirror so we might get a good look at ourselves.

CHAPTER TWO

character: ourselves, close-up

"Let's go on by using new eyes to look into a mirror so we might get a good look at ourselves."

ACTS 27 TELLS THE STORY of the apostle Paul being taken by ship to Rome as a prisoner. Those in charge of the ship found themselves battling difficult sailing conditions, and yet they were in need of a friendly harbor in which to spend the winter. Paul advised them that sailing on would be treacherous, and perhaps even deadly, but those in charge made the decision to press on toward a Cretan harbor called Phoenix. I like how the NIV 1984 phrases the first half of verse 13: "When a gentle south wind began to blow, [the sailors] thought they had obtained what they wanted."

THE GENTLE SOUTH WIND

The initial conditions suggested that they were right and Paul was wrong, so they raised the anchor and made their way toward Phoenix. Let's turn to *The Message*'s paraphrase of verses 14 and 15 to see what happened next: "But they were no sooner out to sea than a gale-force wind, the infamous nor'easter struck. They lost all control of the ship. It was a cork in the storm."

I don't know about you, but I've been there. A gentle south wind blows—opportunity, recognition, reward, temptation—and

I think I've obtained what I wanted. I think I'm finally on my way, that I've stumbled into the optimal conditions for validation or security or satisfaction. But it's not long before a storm rolls in and I've lost all control.

As Acts 27 continues, the ship is pounded by wind and waves. Luke writes, "When neither sun nor stars appeared for many days and the storm continued raging, we finally gave up all hope of being saved" (v. 20). If I'm honest, I've been there, too.

Miraculously, Acts 27 doesn't end with Paul and the others aboard the ship settling into watery graves. Yes, the ship ran aground and the stern was dismantled by the waves, but Luke reports that by swimming or clinging for dear life to pieces of the ship, every member of the voyage made it to land and lived to tell the tale. Thank God I've been there, too.

REVISITING OUR STORIES

Maybe as you read that, a "gentle south wind" story from your past comes to mind. Something came into your life—a relationship, a job, a material possession—and you thought you'd obtained what you wanted. *This is it!* you told yourself and anyone else who would listen. You picked up anchor and set sail, carried on the wings of your newfound prize, which would certainly make you whole. But when the storm hit, you didn't just lose your thing; you lost *everything*. You were undone, clinging for life to a splintered plank and steeling yourself for the end.

I have my "gentle south wind" stories. I've been so deceived as to believe that a certain amount of money would paper over the emptiness in my soul. I've been so foolish as to believe that even close relationships would be an external source of enough joy, affirmation, and security to quiet my anxious heart. I've been naive enough to believe that validation from friends, leaders, and stand-in father figures would provide me with an identity.

As I revisit these stories, they teach me. I learn about my neediness and the kinds of things my neediness prompts me to chase. I learn about my propensity to turn gifts into idols and why God instructs us to have no gods before Him. I learn that not everything in this world that looks like a ladder is capable of supporting my weight. I learn that God is with me when I misstep and when the storm ensues; He is with me when I wash ashore covered in barnacles and burping up salt-water. The story—the character, the objective, the conflict, the resolution—teaches me to better understand the life and self God has given (and is giving) me.

In the story, everything I know and feel and experienced comes together, and it changes me. This book, which I wrote and which bears my name, represents a dream come true for me. And yet, because of the "gentle south wind" stories I've collected in the last ten years, I was less inclined to make an idol of the book contract when I signed it. I hope this doesn't sound arrogant but I think I was able to value the opportunity to write this book rather than derive my value from it. For me, the survivor of many self-imposed shipwrecks, the difference is paramount.

In *The Whole-Brain Child,* authors Daniel Siegel and Tina Payne Bryson write:

> This is what storytelling does: it allows us to understand ourselves and our world by using both our left and right hemispheres together. To tell a story that makes sense, the left hemisphere must put things in order, using words and logic. The right brain contributes the bodily sensations, raw emotions, and personal memories, so we can see the whole picture and communicate our experience. This is the scientific explanation behind why journaling and talking about a difficult event can be so powerful in helping us heal.[1]

The passage above makes a bold claim—that storytelling allows us to understand ourselves—and I believe it to be true. After all, what are we, really? Are we our résumés? Are we the sum of our successes and failures? Are we a composite of our relationships? Are we what we perceive ourselves to be or what others perceive us to be? If we say yes to any of these options, we must admit that who we are is indefinable, intangible, always subject to change.

OUR STORY'S OUTLINE

But what if we are who God says we are? What if He knit each of us together and ordained all our days (Psalm 139)? What if He loved us so much He sent Jesus to save us into new life? What if He directs our steps and marks out a race for us (Hebrews 12:1)? If that's true, then that's the outline of your story. This outline is at the foundation of who you are and who I am. The better we understand the story of God and man in the Bible, the better we'll understand our basic identities. The more we press into our individual stories, the more we'll understand ourselves as individuals, meaning we'll have a truer grasp of where we've been, where we are, and where we might go from here.

> To make meaning, to make sense of what we experience, we need to be storytellers.

There's no use asking, "Who am I?" without looking to story. The raw facts—your height, weight, age, level of education, net worth, etc.—might be all a marketing executive would care to know about you, but the facts alone aren't enough to convey meaning. To make meaning, to make sense of what we experience, we need to be storytellers. Depending on how much chaos, pain, and loss you need to make sense of, you may be required to engage in what Dr. Alan Wolfelt calls *soul work*, "a downward movement in the psyche; a willingness to connect with what is dark, deep, and not necessarily pleasant."[2] Difficult as it may be, the reward is worth the journey.

In *Still,* author Lauren Winner reflects on an ancient Christian story from the days of the desert fathers about a young man seeking a more ascetic life. He had already spent a year meditating in a cave, so he went to his teachers seeking more rigorous practices. The young man is repeatedly advised to return to his cave to spend more time by himself. He doesn't want to return to the cave—he's ready to do something big and dramatic—but his mentors insist that the cave will be what's best for him. "The point, I think," Winner writes, "is that you can't simply pursue God in the desert; you must also begin to pursue yourself. You cannot fast if you have not first noticed that you are hungry; your hunger is what the cave can teach."[3]

For us, the cave is more an activity than a place. The cave is where we do the soul work by sorting out our stories and uncovering a clearer picture of ourselves.

SHARING A TRAUMATIC NARRATIVE

These days we rarely talk about war without mentioning post-traumatic stress disorder, though this wasn't always the case. In fact, mental health is a more significant component of the modern military than most of us realize. A 2011 report published two alarming estimates: First, from 2005 to 2010, the US military lost a service member to suicide once every thirty-six hours. Even worse, according to the US Department of Veterans Affairs a veteran dies by suicide once every eighty minutes.[4]

Clearly, the threat of war extends beyond the battlefield. But why now? Why from these concurrent wars in Iraq and Afghanistan? The US military has engaged in a number of conflicts, so why did the active-duty suicide rate reach an all-time high in 2011?[5]

Child development specialist Dr. Karyn Purvis offers a theory that connects combat trauma with storytelling.

At a conference for adoptive and foster families I heard Dr. Purvis explain how the experience of leaving war has changed for our soldiers in the last seventy years. It used to be that when a soldier was sent home from a tour of duty, he had a long journey ahead of him. In World War II, a soldier in Europe might have taken a Jeep or a truck to a train station. Then he'd take a slow-moving train loaded with other soldiers to a major port. Next, he'd board a massive ship (again loaded with other soldiers) and float west toward America. As the days went by, the soldiers would gather around a table, playing cards into the wee hours of the morning and telling their stories. They'd describe the war from their vantage points, naming the battles and regions where the firefights and shelling had been the most intense. They'd eulogize their fallen brothers.

> By the time a soldier returns to his home in the States, he might not have shared a meaningful story with anyone else.

Somehow as the weeks passed and the stories breathed, the soldiers would collectively heal a little. By the time a World War II veteran made it back to Georgia or Kansas or Ohio, he'd given voice to what he'd been through and he knew he wasn't alone. Even if he never spoke about the war again, even if he never completed the healing process, he had at least had the opportunity to develop a functional peace about it all.

By today's standards, the old soldier's journey seems antiquated. A soldier on leave could get from Iraq to the United States in about two days, although the processing takes longer if the soldier is finishing a tour. Either way, the reality is that in the 21st century, a soldier leaving a war zone travels by plane instead of freighter, and he can spend most of that time with his earbuds in if he prefers. By the time a soldier returns to his home in the States, he might not have shared a meaningful story with anyone else. And given the nature of the chaos he witnessed overseas, he's unlikely to share those stories with family and friends for whom the stories would lack context or a hint of shared experience. It's possible that the effects of circumventing the story exchange process are manifested in a generation of veterans for whom reintegration into American society has been an often painful and sometimes violent undertaking.

When a soldier returns home without telling his story, he experiences the collision of familiar surroundings and unfamiliar feelings. The soldier's story is meant to be the bridge between who he was when he shipped out and who he has now become. Without the bridge of story—a reconciled sense of self—many find themselves trapped on one side of a chasm created by their experiences, unable to cross safely to the other side.

LOSING THE STORY

In cases involving trauma, story is a key component in helping a person recover a sense of self. Trauma can't be accepted until some order is brought to its chaos. Once ordered or organized to some degree, traumatic narratives can be rehearsed, revisited, and even shared. Each of these is unpleasant, but they further diminish the chaos, thereby making room for perspective, empathy, and acceptance.

If the idea of a sense of self sounds abstract (or more bluntly, like New Age psychobabble), let's consider specific kinds of people we might describe as severely lacking a sense of self. Imagine someone with a profound case of amnesia. You could teach that person the facts about their life, and yet even if they memorized those facts anew, they might still wonder, "Who am I?" They'll both ask and be unable to answer because their stories are gone.

Have you ever had a conversation with a friend or relative suffering from Alzheimer's or dementia? In my experience, the unpredictable vacillation between utter certainty and utter confusion is uniquely unsettling. Watching someone you love gradually lose their stories—and in the process, themselves—is tragic. We think, "Boy, my body is one thing, but when my mind starts to go . . ." and we're worried about something far more important than our ability to solve a crossword puzzle. To the extent that we've got a grip on our stories, we've got a grip on our sense of self. The frightening prospect of losing that grip ought to point us toward the value of going deeper into our stories, leaving no stone unturned, and helping others do the same.

SAYING "I WAS . . ."

The power of narrative starts with the beauty of the words "I was." Those words signify that we have a past (as we all do) and that we've come to terms with it (as only some of us do). Those words signify that we have a story to tell, and as we know, stories involve conflict. When we say, "I was . . ." (and then tell the truth) we're acknowledging that we've experienced things we'd rather not have experienced and that we've been people we'd rather not have been.

Maybe you'd say, "I was a fatherless kid who had a tendency to turn his inward self-loathing outward onto others." Maybe you'd say, "I was so prideful and narcissistic that I threw away my career with a single mistake." Maybe you'd say you were abandoned, deceived, hurt, imprisoned, robbed, or bullied. Maybe you'd say you were an addict, an abuser, a people-pleaser, a liar, a thief, an adulterer, or any number of other things. Whatever your particular backstory—whatever the depth or origin of your hardships—can you own it? Can you name it? Can you organize it and articulate it? And finally, have you been delivered from it? That's not to say you're perfect, but to borrow Kurt Vonnegut's phrasing, you're not stuck at the bottom of the "hole" anymore.

When Christians say "I was," we're acknowledging more than where we've been; we're remembering what God has done for us and in us through Christ.

THE "I" STORY

Tim Keller, preaching about the end of the book of Jonah, observes that the final chapter ends rather abruptly. In fact, the book ends with God asking the still-obstinate Jonah a rhetorical question: "And should I not have concern for the great city of Nineveh, in which there are more than a hundred and twenty thousand people who cannot tell their right hand from their left—and also many animals?" And that's it. End of book. We're left wondering what became of Jonah—did he ever come around?

He came around, Keller concludes.[6] After all, how else would we know about God's repeated calls to Jonah, Jonah's petulance, and the prophet-gobbling beast? At some point after God's rhetorical question, Jonah must have begun to see the world the way God sees it, and then he wrote down his story for us. Thankfully, he didn't soft-pedal his flaws. Instead, he left us plenty to learn about ourselves and our nature. As Keller points out, Jonah isn't even the protagonist of the story that bears his name. Rather, the prophet is honest enough to admit he was the antagonist in God's plan to reach out to the people of Nineveh. But Jonah didn't remain an antagonist; he became a storyteller. The story he told was an "I was" story that has echoed for centuries.

The apostle Paul told his own "I was" story across several of his letters. He was dead in sin (Romans 7:9) and he persecuted the church (1 Corinthians 15:9, Galatians 1:13). He confessed he was "a blasphemer and a persecutor and a violent man," ignorant and unbelieving (1 Timothy 1:13). Paul persecuted the church, but then Jesus got ahold of him and used him to influence the shape of the church forever. *There's* a story.

In Paul's letters, he also helps his readers with their stories. Instead of "I was," Paul says, "You were":

> As for you, *you were* dead in your transgressions and sins, in which you used to live when you followed the ways of this world . . . But because of his great love for us, God, who is rich in mercy, made us alive with Christ . . . Ephesians 2:1–2, 4–5 (emphasis mine).

We find another great example in 1 Corinthians 6, in which Paul rattles off a list of what he calls "wrongdoers," a series of identities Paul says "will not inherit the kingdom of God" (v. 9). After the list, lest his readers be tempted toward moral superiority, Paul grounds them in their common story: "And that is what some of *you were*. But you were washed, you were sanctified, you were justified in the name of the Lord Jesus Christ and by the Spirit of our God" (v. 11).

The best part is that the specifics of you all belong in the story.

There's a story—*our story*. It's a story that grounds us in who we were and how we were saved from our former selves. The more we internalize this narrative, the more we see ourselves for who we really are. This is the story in which our identity leaps off the page and demands to be seen and heard and felt and believed.

This washed-sanctified-justified story is bigger than you or me, and wonderfully so. It's cosmos big. It's the story under and over your story. It's the story behind and in front of your story. The redemption narrative undergirds our lives with a shared perspective, hope, and love.

The best part is that the specifics of you—your unique and proprietary blend of gifts, talents, struggles, scars, desires, foibles, and the way you mispronounce certain words—they all belong in the story. Don't edit them out; leave them in. They belong the same way Paul's specifics were undeniably relevant as he ministered and taught through his letters—just go back to his "I was" passages if you don't believe me. Your story matters because you matter. You matter because God made you.

THE TWELVE STEPS

I once heard someone talk a little bit about the legacy of Bill Wilson, the founder of Alcoholics Anonymous. Wilson's relationship to alcohol was so intense he described the first time he got drunk from a few cocktails as discovering "the elixir of life." Alcohol steered Wilson to professional ruin and hospitalization, and it wasn't until he had a profound spiritual experience that he was able to practice sobriety in earnest. From there he was compelled to do what he could to help other alcoholics experience freedom, and a few years later the movement was born.

In listening to Wilson's story, I began to think about my perception of Alcoholics Anonymous (as well as its evangelical offspring, Celebrate Recovery) as an organization that helps people find healing. There's certainly more to the program and the Twelve Steps than I realize, but there's something distinctive about people in recovery: they know their stories and they tell them.

The Twelve Steps contain a number of propositions participants must accept and admissions they must make. The first of these, Step One, requires participants to acknowledge their lives had become unmanageable. But this admission isn't coerced or compelled in isolation. Rather, "My life had become unmanageable," is meant to be a conclusion drawn from the individual's story of addiction and self-destruction. The Twelve Steps are powerful in their insistence that people come to terms with the depths of their addictions and commit themselves to the healing process.

The more we pay attention to our stories—the more we listen—the more we hear the truth about ourselves. Your story proclaims that you are the work of the Great Artist. His signature is present in the story itself. When we're secure in that truth, we find the freedom to tell our story to others who are willing to listen.

RETELLING AND HEALING

Early in *The Whole-Brain Child*, Siegel and Bryson discuss how the mother of a two-year-old helped her son come to terms with a frightening car accident. "That night and the next week, when Marco's mind continually brought him back to the car crash, *Marianna helped him retell the story over and again*"[7] (emphasis mine). But why would a mother continually engage a toddler with a potentially traumatizing story? The authors rightly acknowledge that many of us would be tempted to change the subject as quickly as possible, even through the use of ice cream if necessary. "In allowing Marco to repeatedly retell the story," Siegel and Bryson conclude, "Marianna was helping him understand what had happened so he could begin to deal with it emotionally."[8]

The difference between Marianna's approach and the way I would approach a similarly intense situation (avoidance and ice cream) suggests that I confuse emotional distance with emotional resolution. Distance is the shortcut, the quickest way to relief, and we achieve it by suppressing what we feel and distracting ourselves with lighter fare. Distance requires an investment of effort up front, but eventually, we do experience the relief we sought. It's not unlike a last-minute cram session before an exam—we may pass the test in the short-term, but we haven't learned anything. The opportunity for growth in the form of knowledge, self-awareness, internalization, and healing slips away like whatever names, dates, and vocabulary words we scribbled on our stack of flash cards. Distance is a cheap substitute for perspective and closure—it enables us to numb the turmoil, and it encourages us to interpret the observable absence of turmoil as the presence of peace.

Resolution is the real object, and resolution is only available through some measure of understanding. When we can construct the narrative using facts and feelings, when we can begin to recognize cause and effect relationships, when we can acknowledge that we survived the ordeal somehow, we've managed a bit of resolution through story. Even better, when we sketch out our stories with God in mind, we see His grace, goodness, and faithfulness emerge from the pages.

> Distance is a cheap substitute for perspective and closure.

Near the end of Ian Cron's memoir, *Jesus, My Father, the CIA, and Me,* the author connects his turbulent childhood to the anxiety he experiences as a father. In one anecdote, Cron recounts his intense reaction to the prospect of his children jumping off the highest cliff at a local swimming hole. His wife can't help but wonder why he's so adamantly against it. Here's his recollection of their conversation:

> "Forty feet is a long way to fall," I said.
>
> Anne's face softened, and she placed her hand on my cheek. "Ian, they're not falling; they're jumping."
>
> I had trouble sleeping that night. I couldn't help thinking about what Anne had said about the difference between the kids jumping and falling. My childhood had been an emotional and spiritual free fall. Often there was no net, no soft landing in the water with a parent waiting, and I got hurt.[9]

It's in this passage that Cron reveals the healing power of memoir. By doing the work of telling our own stories, we acknowledge the ways we've been shaped—for better and worse—by where we've been and who we've been with. We acknowledge the character we've become and are becoming. In Cron's case, identifying the source of his anxiety was the beginning of freedom from it, at least as it pertained to his kids and the cliff.

Our pasts have a way of maintaining a grip on our presents, whether we realize it or not. If we're willing to piece together our stories and see the relationships between what happened *then* and what's happening *now,* we get to make choices about what happens *next.* What I mean is that we get to decide what to do with our anxiety, pain, trust issues, addictions, and so on—do we want to be at their beck and call forever or do we want to take them on? I can't say I hold the secret to overcoming any of those particular struggles, but I can say that sketching the story you want to tell going forward is the first step.

We don't have to do anything more to earn God's love or salvation. But like any healthy relationship, when we're in love with God, wouldn't it be fun to go on an adventure with Him? I see this at work in my relationship with my daughter. It's not enough for my daughter and me to just be in the same room. "Dad," she says with a spark, "let's *do something together."*

Whenever she says it, her eyes are alive with possibility, and I can't turn her away. So we enter into this process where we're both searching our minds and our surroundings for the thing, just the right thing, for us. We don't always find just the right thing, but when we do we know it.

I think this is a hint of what it looks like when we write our stories with God.

narrator: God

"We don't always find just the right thing, but when we do we know it. I think this is a hint of what it looks like when we write our stories with God."

WHEN I WAS FOUR OR five, I believed my Sunday school teacher when she talked about God. She talked about God like He was real, like He was *around,* and I believed those things. I even believed God went to our church in Fort Worth, Texas, and roamed the halls on Sundays like hundreds of other adults. I believed this because I thought I saw Him every week.

A PICTURE OF JESUS

I assume the children's wing of the church I attended growing up was representative of every church's children's wing in the mid-1980s. There were cream-colored cinder block walls, hallways of dingy orange carpet, and bulletin boards covered in haphazard arts and crafts. In the foyer there was an enormous fish tank, an unironic paisley sofa, and above that, a four-foot-wide painting of the scene in Matthew 19 and Luke 18 in which Jesus told the disciples to let the children come to Him.

The painting featured Jesus as I'd come to know Him—white, clean, and handsome—taking a knee in the midst of a diverse gang of little rascals. He's smiling, naturally, adorned by a thin white halo and undisturbed by the germs and persistent questions that tend to accompany small children. He also had the standard shoulder-length brown hair and neatly trimmed beard.

I looked at the painting every Sunday, so I had a pretty good idea what Jesus looked like. Imagine my surprise, then, the first time I saw a man in the children's wing who looked about twenty-five years older than Jesus, smiling and surrounded by children who were excited to see him. Instead of long hair, he had a shiny bald head and short brown hair on the sides. Instead of a beard, the man had a mustache like Gerald McRaney from *Major Dad*. But the resemblance to the Jesus in the painting was undeniable, and that's when it dawned on me:

Ooooh, that guy must be Jesus's dad! God goes to our church!

My Sunday school teacher was right—God was around.

I don't know exactly when I stopped believing in Bald Mustache God, but I guess I moved on to a different picture. I've latched on to several different versions of God in the twenty-five years since I believed He was a friendly guy in a Cosby sweater next to the fish tank in the children's wing. There was Santa God, Grandpa God, Indifferent God, Wizard of Oz God, Bob Knight God, Tim the Enchanter[1] God, and others.

What I mean to say is that I've always had a picture of God in my mind, and maybe you're the same way. More often than not, the picture I was using at a given time was shaped by what I'd recently seen, heard, or experienced, and yet no picture really did the trick. None of them stuck. I think this is because while I apparently needed to know who God was, I didn't know where to look.

I respect you too much to pretend I have God figured out now, but I think I'm learning to look in the right places. Just as listening to a person's story is vital to understanding who they are, God offers us His story so that we can see Him being Himself.

KID STUFF

We raise our children in the church by teaching them the stories. Sure, we often edit these stories to deemphasize the drowning and the smiting and the circumcising, but the point is we start them off with the stories. Maybe this is because we don't believe their attention spans could handle our grown-up principles and formulas for upright living, or maybe it's simply that we recognize the value in teaching children that God is real and involved with humanity.

Perhaps we recognize the value in teaching children that Jesus is more than an idea or a source of Tweet-worthy tidbits, but rather He is God who took on flesh, was born to a virgin, and walked the earth. We want our children to know Jesus was betrayed, crucified, and buried, only to be raised to life by the Father. We want our children to know these things, and so we tell them the stories. We have

> "The gospel is not advice to be lived up to, it's a story to be lived into."

them act it out, we have them sing songs, and we have them color pictures because we want them to internalize these stories and believe them in their heart of hearts.

I love the perspective of respected children's author Sally Lloyd-Jones:

"I wrote *The Jesus Storybook Bible* so children could meet the Hero in its pages. And become part of His Magnificent Story. Because rules don't change you. But a Story—God's Story—can."[2]

Now, tell me, at what age should we set these stories aside and focus on the principles? I once heard my friend Barry Jones say during a sermon, "The gospel is not advice to be lived up to, it's a story to be lived into."[3]

Yes.

Maybe the problem is that a pastor has to stand before an American evangelical church and explicitly state that truth. The pastor has to say this because of our tendency toward the advice approach. When presented with two options—an undomesticated and certainly unsafe adventure; or a list of twenty-seven character traits to be studied and discussed over Styrofoam cups of Folgers Classic Roast—many of us choose the morality study. Especially since our eternal destiny has already been secured.

But the story is where we find the real stuff.

THE REVEAL

Every great story hinges on the choices the characters make. Think about your favorite TV show (please don't let it be anything about sexy doctors and sassy nurses). Setting and genre and aesthetics are important, but once you're in the middle of it, the characters and the choices they make are what captivate us. If that's the case, we have a major clue as to why the story of God in the Bible is important—because it reveals choices, and choices reveal character. Through the choices people make in the Bible's pages we can learn volumes about ourselves and our nature. More important, God's story reveals His character and makes it available to us. Through the choices God makes we see the depth and breadth of His beauty, creativity, holiness, justness, and grace.

In *With*, author Skye Jethani considers two tests professor Scot McKnight gives to Bible college students who take his course on Jesus. The first test asks the students what they think about Jesus' personality, while the second test asks each student about his or her personality. It may come as a surprise—or sadly, maybe not—but most students perceive Jesus as having a personality remarkably similar to their own.[4] In other words, we might say that we all have an unconscious tendency to baptize our particular dispositions by projecting them onto the God of the universe.

I don't know about you, but I'd say that's a problem. What's the solution? While there is no easy cure for our ingrained worship of self, I can't help but think immersing ourselves in God's story is a logical place to start. After all, the story reveals the Storyteller, and therefore its value is paramount.

It may be that one of the most faithful things we can do is take God's story just as it's given to us, in its fullness and entirety. We breathe in the fullness of this story because it is the biggest of big pictures the beginning, middle, and end of God's creation and re-creation project.

It's both His labor and the fruit of the labor.

The big picture provides context all along the way, through the events and the generations and the covenants. We read the creation story knowing things will go wrong. We read about sin, suffering, and injustice knowing things will be made right. Whenever we engage a specific event in the story, from the flood to the Ten Commandments to the Acts of the Apostles, the big picture is always instructive. The fullness of the story illuminates why God reached out to Abraham to begin setting apart a people for Himself through whom He would bless the nations. And later in the story we see the magnificence of the Abraham plotline revealed in Jesus. Even after Jesus ascends, the story sheds more light on the kingdom He came to announce and the shape of the cosmic reconciliation He mediated. At the beginning of the story, He made all things; at its denouement, He will make all things new.

> At the beginning of the story, He made all things; at its denouement, He will make all things new.

In seeking to understand God through narrative, we're seeking *more*—more than our limited experiences, more than our present emotions, more than a grandfatherly abstraction, more than a list of prohibitions and obligations. We're seeking His person.

What I mean is that in His story we find Him. We find His creativity, compassion, justice, tenderness, firmness, mercy, strength, holiness, persistence, mysteriousness, and so much more as they bear themselves out in the choices He makes.

As we soak in these things, we affirm in our minds not just *who God is,* but that He is a *who* in the first place. His story persuades us He is good. He is active. He is near. As Skye Jethani observed, the focus of both the garden at the beginning and the Holy City at the end is God's relationship with humanity. "This is why God created us," he writes, "and it is the end to which all of history is marching."[5]

IN EDEN AND EGYPT AND . . .

Sean Gladding wrote a wonderful book called *The Story of God, the Story of Us,* and the title fits. Gladding's work is a moving presentation of the events of the Bible as a long-form narrative. The Old Testament arc is recounted by an elder statesman among a band of Jews disillusioned by their exile to Babylon in the sixth century BC. From Sabbath to Sabbath, the people gather around the fire as the old man gives them the next installment of the story.[6] The storyteller's reasoning for sharing the story with his alienated friends, family, and neighbors is insightful:

> "I understand," the old man continues, "why you may believe that God has forsaken us. But we are still God's people, and we are part of a Story that did not begin with exile, nor with the Babylonians. We are far from home; indeed, we are a long way east of Eden . . . I understand that you want answers. But what we have is a Story, which I would have you hear from the beginning."[7]

Gladding's first New Testament narrator is a woman whose home is a meeting place for a first-century church. She saw Jesus ride into Jerusalem on a donkey and continued to bear witness to His story. The second narrator is an inhabitant of Rome who is all too familiar with the increasing persecution of the early church at the hands of the Empire. Like the Old Testament arc, the events of the New Testament are told to an audience of people who need to find their bearings in confusing times. The author's implication is that just as the story of God served to ground people in millennia past, so it also may ground us in the millennia to come.

The beauty of *The Story of God, the Story of Us* and its ability to illuminate God's heart for humanity shed some light on our piecemeal approach to the Bible. We would never read *The Catcher in the Rye* the way we often read the Bible. We would never focus on the scene in which Holden sneaks into his family's apartment to the exclusion of the scenes that preceded it. If we did, we'd have no idea why a

> Though the Bible's cast of characters is extensive, God is always central.

boy would feel the need to sneak into his home in the first place. We would never focus on a sentence of dialogue spoken between Holden and Phoebe to the exclusion of the context in which it was uttered. And yet we engage the Bible this way with alarming regularity. As such, Gladding's book is unique among the scores of Christian books published each year.

Encountering God's story as He has given it to us teaches us some important things about faith. For one thing, as the times and places and people change, the story marches on. In other words, the size and continuity of the story far transcend any one human life despite our preference to view life and history on these terms. God's unfolding project is so expansive it shames our megalomania.

The story also trains us to believe in the presence of God. Though the Bible's cast of characters is extensive, God is always central. He is always present. He was there in Eden and Babel and Egypt and Jerusalem and Nineveh and Bethlehem and Gethsemane and Rome and Patmos, whether or not the supporting actors acknowledged Him. Even now we live and move and have our being in Him, for He is not far from any one of us (Acts 17:27–28). His story is insistent upon this truth.

God's story is always about the pursuit of or interaction with people. When Adam and Eve hid in the wake of their rebellion and strung together fig leaves to alleviate their naked shame, God sought them out. When humanity hid in darkness, God's love of the hiding ones moved Him to offer Himself in the person of His Son as a means of reconciliation. So how does God feel about you and your seven billion neighbors? Rather than remaining content to merely post a mission statement on the wall, His story demonstrates His mission time and again.

THE BIG STORY

Scot McKnight, the professor I mentioned earlier in this chapter, explores how we ought to understand the gospel in his book *The King Jesus Gospel: The Original Good News Revisited*, and he finds God's story is essential.

"The gospel only makes sense in [the Bible's] story," he writes. McKnight continues: "Now a very important claim: without that story there is no gospel. This leads to a second claim: if we ignore that story, the gospel gets distorted, and that is just what has happened in salvation cultures."[8]

What McKnight is doing is contrasting modern evangelicalism's pray-the-prayer-and-cross-the-sin-divide gospel with the gospel of the New Testament, and he finds the current model wanting for a lack of narrative.

The authentic apostolic gospel, the gospel Paul received and passed on and the one the Corinthians received, concerns these events in the life of Jesus:

> *that Christ died,*
> *that Christ was buried,*
> *that Christ was raised,*
> *and that Christ appeared.*

The gospel is the story of the crucial events in the life of Jesus Christ. Scot McKnight cautions us about not paying enough attention to the setting and context of the gospel when we consider its truths. I stand with him when he deplores our reduction of God's gospel to "the abstract, de-storified points in the Plan of Salvation,"[9] not because I don't believe in the saving power of Jesus Christ, but rather because I believe God knew what He was doing when He married the gospel to a story. God chose a particular story, and so the story must be good for us. The true nature of our calling to new life in Christ must be a narrative in which a character who wants something overcomes conflict in order to get it, rather than a self-help sales pitch or a progression of logical proofs.

Without the big story, the cross is just a shape, an intersection, a pair of wooden beams. Without the big story, the Crucifixion is just the torture and murder of an innocent man. Without the big story, the Christian life is merely an obligation to morality now in exchange for heaven later. But with the big story, we see Jesus as the most pivotal part of the drama that began in the garden and will resolve in the Holy City. As I argued earlier, the story is thick with mission.

The night Jesus was betrayed, He gave His disciples food and drink. He explained that the bread and the wine were His body and His blood, given for them, and He instructed them to remember as often as they partook. It seems that even before Jesus went to the cross He was calling His disciples to establish a rhythm of returning to the story. Let's examine two specific stories I think capture the inviting of what God is doing in history.

HOSEA'S STORY

The Bible includes the writings of several prophets, but Hosea was something of a special case. Whereas Jeremiah only had to walk down to the potter's house to receive a message from the Lord in the form of an object lesson (Jeremiah 18), Hosea had to walk down the aisle. More specifically, Hosea had to *go marry a promiscuous woman and have children with her* (Hosea 1:2). Hosea had to *become* the object lesson so God could communicate truth about Himself and our wandering hearts. I don't know about you but I find it endlessly fascinating that God called Hosea into a personal story that represented the broader story of God and Israel. In the story, Hosea must repeatedly pursue his wayward wife just as God repeatedly pursues His people. If we can admit our propensity to wander, the relentless grace in Hosea's story is nothing short of good news.

> In God's story we find that the lost need not stay lost, the sick need not stay sick, and the runaways need not stay away.

The final chapter of Hosea is ripe with hope for the story going forward. God says, "I will heal their waywardness and love them freely, for my anger has turned away from them" (Hosea 14:4). In God's story we find that the lost need not stay lost, the sick need not stay sick, and the runaways need not stay away. That's the story whether you believe it or not.

God went to great lengths to model redemption in the life of one of His prophets, but that pales in comparison to the lengths

God went to in enacting redemption in the lives of His people. If we miss redemption as a recurring thread in God's story, we've missed the story. While Hosea's story is explicitly about the reclamation of a wandering lover, this is hardly an isolated theme. The original lovers wandered—as has every human being since—but God's love never fails. The story tells us that.

LEVI'S STORY

In Mark 2:14 we find Jesus walking by a tax collector's booth manned by Levi son of Alphaeus. As you may know, tax collectors were reviled in first-century Israel. For one thing, tax collectors worked on behalf of the Roman Empire, the violent pagan occupying force that made God's chosen people a subjugated nation. Also, a tax collector made his living by gouging citizens above and beyond Rome's designated tax burdens. So Levi, a Jew, worked for Rome and took advantage of his fellow Jews. I can only imagine how Jesus might have laid into Levi.

Jesus could have yelled about Levi's sin—the guy was a liar and a cheater and he probably skipped Sunday school more often than not. Jesus could have threatened Levi with hell, which we all know will include a special wing for tax collectors. Jesus could

> Levi stepped into a new story, one brimming with the full life.

have taken Levi on an epic guilt trip for his role in the institutional mistreatment and marginalization of his own tribe. But Jesus didn't do any of those things. Instead, he offered Levi a better story.

As Mark tells it, all Jesus said was, "Follow me." It's only two words, but those words imply a story. They mark the beginning of an epic journey. Whereas sometimes we focus on condemning people's present stories, with Levi Jesus was content to focus on the invitation into a new story. I think this scene and others like it from the Gospels teach us that Jesus is not as fixated on perpetrating shame as we are. Shame doesn't seem to serve His purposes the way we believe it will serve ours. But what are His purposes?

"I have come that they may have life, and have it to the full," he declared (John 10:10). It was this full life that Jesus extended to Levi, knowing perfectly well that the less-than-full life had left him empty. I wonder what would happen if we let the calling of Levi in Mark 2 convince us of God's disposition toward the tax collectors and sinners. As Jesus explains just two verses later, He specifically came to call people like Levi, and call is what He did.

"Follow me," Jesus said. Levi stood to his feet and stepped into a new story, one brimming with the full life—joyful communion with Christ and community with others—that awaits all those who are willing to stand up from their tables and follow Him.

LET'S GO

Earlier I said story is about pursuit. Story is movement by a character or group of characters from one point (physical, emotional, or otherwise) to another point. A story is progress, action toward an outcome. We might frame "Follow me," then, as meaning, "Let's go. Let's tell a story together."

Samuel Wells wrote, "The saint is just a small character in a story that's always fundamentally about God."[10] The thing about the story about God is that He always seems to invite new saints into it. He's always saying, "Let's go," not blocking the way. Even the word *repent* in the New Testament isn't meant to be a barrier between the pious and the heathens—it's a plea to you to change your mind. When Jesus and His apostles said, "Repent," they were saying, "Stop following that and start following *this.*" *Repent* is an invitation to a story exchange.

When we understand the gospel and the Christian life as a story, we get a sense that we're called to something more than an ideology, a bundle of good behaviors, and an "Admit One" ticket to heaven. It's a story, but not the kind your sophomore English teacher assigned—meaning it's not a story to skim or avoid or study at arm's length with academic detachment. We're not consumers of the gospel; far from it.

God gives us His story that we might get a glimpse of who He is. But He doesn't stop there. God extends to us a story to enter, a story to put on, a story to tell.

objective: make something

"When we understand the gospel and the Christian life as a story, we get a sense that we're called to something more than an ideology or a bundle of good behaviors."

IN A COMMENCEMENT ADDRESS AT a Christian university, artist and author Makoto Fujimura repeatedly asked the new graduates, "What do you want to make today?"[1]

Fujimura's question is more often asked of kindergartners than twenty-two-year-olds, but it communicates a vital truth to both age groups: the future is teeming with possibility if you're willing to tell a good story. As I said in chapter 1, story is movement by a character or group of characters from one point (physical, emotional, or otherwise) to another point. A story is progress, action toward an outcome. Whether you're 5, 25, or 105 years old, the question "What do you want to make today?" points you toward an object, which is the starting place for story. Story is not only a source of rear-facing revelation, as was our focus in chapter 2; story also looks forward. *Where am I going from here?* is just another way of asking, *What story am I going to tell?*

Without asking a question like Fujimura's, without attempting to sketch out the beginnings of a good story, it's difficult to take a purposeful step. A story goes something like, "I want to teach children to express themselves through art," or "I want to start a company that contributes to, rather than squeezes, its community." Without an objective, there is no progress. Why? Because by definition, there's nothing to progress toward. You can stand still, you can step out in a random direction, or you can blindly follow someone else's path, but you can't begin the rest of your work life without a story.

So. What do you want to make today?

WORTHY STORIES

In his letter to the Ephesians (which we'll talk more about later in this chapter), Paul offered a lofty standard for the choices we make: "I urge you to live a life worthy of the calling you have received" (4:1). While he wasn't speaking specifically about work or objective, but of our lives on the whole, the standard seems fitting. Whatever stories we choose to tell, they ought to be worthy. Paul knew the calling we've received is the truest measure of a life, and as such, it's not enough to simply self-identify as a story-teller—our stories must be worthy.

The great director Frank Capra knew what it meant to tell a worthwhile story. He wrote, "There are no rules in filmmaking, only sins. And the cardinal sin is Dullness."[2] In other words, the objective must be meaningful, the characters must be determined, and the outcome must be in doubt. Otherwise, the result is a dull and decidedly unworthy story.

MINISTRY AND MARKETPLACE

One day I got an email from a web developer in Sweden named Tobias. Tobias helps churches with their websites, and he was planning a trip to the States that would include a few days in Dallas. When we finally got to meet, we spent a couple hours talking about the church in America and Europe. I left that conversation grateful for the reminder that the church is so much bigger—and so much more diverse—than my paradigm. I also left challenged by a church Tobias told me about in Ukraine, but first I need to tell you about growing up in Texas.

As a teenager who was introduced to the faith at a church that was closely aligned with the seminary down the road, it's fair to say I developed a skewed view of the relationship between faith and vocation. Somehow I learned to associate full-time ministry and long-term missions as sacred, while "secular" or "marketplace" work was merely utilitarian—a necessary evil that provided for families and funded church work through tithing. You can imagine why I spent my college years, surrounded by future youth ministers at a Christian university, agonizing over whether or not I was meant to go to seminary even though I didn't feel God calling me to do so. I wish I'd known about how this church in Ukraine views vocation.

> It's through this approach that the church teaches its people to integrate, rather than separate, their careers and their faith.

As Tobias explained it to me, the church doesn't elevate ministry above the marketplace. Rather, it's all mission work. If you want to be a banker, you have the church's blessing. And you also have the church's commission—you're expected to be a pastor to the banking industry. It's through this approach that the church teaches its people to integrate, rather than separate, their careers and their faith. God is with us as we work, guiding us, sustaining us, and empowering us to be His ambassadors at every level of every industry.

If our working lives will span four or five decades, and if we're going to spend one-third of our waking hours at work, we must tell a story with our work that supersedes compensation, status, and ego. When and where and how we work matters. Why? Because our stories matter, and work is something we were always meant to do.

James Davison Hunter writes that in our work, our creating and cultivating, "we mirror God's own generative act and thus reflect our very nature as ones made in his likeness. In the Christian view, then, human beings are, by divine intent and their very nature, world-makers." The implication, as Hunter observes, is that work is meant for much more than passing the time: "People fulfill their individual and collective destiny in the art, music, literature, commerce, law, and scholarship they cultivate, the relationships they build, and in the institutions they develop—the families, churches, associations, and communities they live in and sustain— as they reflect the good of God and his designs for flourishing."[3]

AS THE SAPLING GROWS

Genesis 2:6 says there was a time when no plant life had yet grown upon the earth, so "streams came up from the earth and watered the whole surface of the ground." Then God planted a garden and brought forth all kinds of life from it—"trees that were pleasing to the eye and good for food"—but the garden, although *good*, wasn't *done*. God also set humanity in the garden with a distinct purpose, a specific story, in mind: "The Lord God took the man and put him in the Garden of Eden to work it and take care of it" (v. 15).

In the beginning, God created mankind on purpose. Humanity, made in the image of the triune God and without sin, had a job to do. Work, in and of itself, is not a result of the post-fall curse like sickness or the lines at the DMV. Rather, as we read the curse in Genesis 3, it seems as though God is explaining how work is about to get much more difficult for the man and woman. From that point forward, work would be marked by toil and sweat.

In the garden, trees were generous with their fruit; outside the garden, the ground would prove stingy. In the same way, perhaps childbirth was always part of the plan, but the curse amounts to God's pronouncement that pain was to become an inexorable part of the process. (Imagine work without struggle and childbearing without all the unpleasant and unsavory aspects! Thanks, Adam and Eve.)

As it is, we work and we struggle. But we ought not interpret the struggle as a sign that we weren't created to work. We were always meant to envision the fruit of our labor, the way we'd envision a sapling becoming a great tree, fully grown and productive and life-giving. We were always meant to be guided by the vision as we prepared the ground, planted the seed, nurtured the emerging stem, and waited for the fruit to burst forth in its due time. We were never in complete control of this process—God always mysteriously shepherded nature's external workings (sunlight, rain) and the plant's internal workings (osmosis, photosynthesis)—but we were always meant to be active participants in it. We tell the story and we play our part in it even if we do not author and orchestrate its action and outcomes. We work.

If we can accept that truth, we need only look at our individual stories to see that our God-given uniqueness shapes our perceptions of and successes within various roles and pursuits. To that end, as God guides us through our stories in the ever-advancing present, He's also helping us construct a scouting report for the future. Nothing made this more apparent to me than my first job out of college.

MAYBE I'M GOING TO BE . . .

They say those who can't do, teach. But what about those who can't teach? They become academic advisors. Okay, that's not fair. What I should have said is I became an academic advisor when I realized I had good grades but not much else—no qualifications, no certifications, no training, and no idea what to do with my life. Thankfully, I found a position at a local university advising undergraduate students who didn't exactly have their career paths charted either.

The year I spent as an academic advisor gave me the opportunity to try my hand in higher education, consider other career options, and spend a lot of time alone in my windowless office reflecting on the person I wanted to become. I also got to sit across the desk from students whose myriad anxieties were largely familiar to me. Often when I gave them advice about college and career, I was really talking to myself, a twenty-two-year-old kid who was only six months into what might be a fifty-year professional odyssey.

> Failure doesn't devalue us or diminish our potential. Instead, this is what happens when the story we're pursuing is incongruous with the story for which we were made.

Ironically, at a time when I was struggling to find my niche, the most difficult students to work with were those who knew exactly what they wanted to do. *I'm going to be an engineer. I'm going to be a nurse. I'm going to be a doctor. I'm going to be a financial analyst.* Whenever I heard a declaration like that, I'd instinctively take a deep breath and brace myself for the conversation that would follow. In all likelihood, very few of those "I'm going to be" statements came true.

I say that because I was part of a team of advisors who worked with undeclared students. Some of those students—the group I could identify with—were undeclared by choice. They were freshmen and sophomores who were still weighing their options and trying out different introductory courses before officially declaring a major and plotting out a degree plan.

The other undeclared students were not undeclared by choice. Instead, they'd received a letter saying they'd been dropped from the business school or the nursing program or the biology department because of low academic performance. The letter told the students to report to my office when they were ready to register for classes, and so they'd come in and insist they were still going to be engineers, nurses, doctors, and financial analysts. They weren't ready to think about career alternatives yet—they were determined to win back the majors that had spurned them. I'm sure some of them succeeded toward this end, but most of them did not.

I realize I might sound negative, but the academic dissonance between these students' plans and abilities presents a few practical problems. If an aspiring engineer can't pass Calculus II or Advanced Physics, do you want to drive on the bridge he builds? If an aspiring nurse or doctor earns a D in Anatomy and Physiology, do you want her making an assessment about your abdominal pain? If an aspiring financial analyst can't make the cut in a junior-level banking class, do you want her making decisions that affect the retirement accounts of thousands of people?

No, you don't.

Each of the students who remained insistent about their desired major was pursuing a story—there was a character, an objective, and conflict all along the way. But most of these stories were fantasies. Based on some of the chaotic transcripts I saw, the fantasies might as well have included hobbits. When someone can only see themselves as something that doesn't remotely fit with their actual potential, there's an obvious problem. A story problem.

Look, this isn't a judgment on anyone who has ever fallen short of a dream or a goal—God knows I have—because failure doesn't devalue us or diminish our potential. Instead, this is what happens when the story we're pursuing is incongruous with the story for which we were made.

A NARRATIVE VIEW OF WORK

As we'll talk about in the next chapter, resistance is not necessarily a sign that we must turn around. Rather, our challenge as characters and storytellers is to discern what choice to make in the face of the resistance. It just so happens that work is an area in which this choice, at least at a high level, is somewhat simple. Where you're interested but not particularly gifted or talented, you're likely to be a great fan. Where you're gifted or talented but not particularly interested, you're likely to be bored. Where your interests overlap with your gifts and talents, you're likely to do great work.

That philosophy isn't particularly revelatory, I know, but it seems to hold true for a lot of people. What it hints at is the importance of self-awareness, meaning that if we can coherently organize the past and honestly evaluate the present, we're well-equipped to sketch out the narrative going forward.

The apostle Paul told the Galatians, "If anyone thinks they are something when they are not, they deceive themselves" (6:3). And while I don't think he had engineers and nurses in mind when he wrote those words, they're no less true. Whether we think we're better than others (Paul's original point) or we think we can simply will our way into an M.D., we're deceiving ourselves.

If we're to take a healthy, narrative view of work, we have to shed the self-deception. We also have to untangle ourselves from the unworthy objectives hidden inside our unrealistic objectives: parents (engineer!), perception (doctor!), and money (financial analyst!). Back when I was working with students, those hidden objectives tended to be at the root of many of these academic careers stuck at the crossroads between stories that *sound* good and stories that are good.

I wasn't long into my advising career when I realized higher education wasn't for me. So while I still had a world of choices before me, I'd managed to cross off one possibility on the list. I eventually found a new position at a new organization, but I still had no idea what I wanted. I still had to wrestle with Fujimura's question: What do you want to make today?

CHOOSING THE OBJECTIVE

Although we Christians manage to differ in our understandings of God's sovereignty and free will, I think—*think*—we all agree that we make choices. Most of us can acknowledge, and even celebrate, God's real and active presence in the world without tumbling into what G.K. Chesterton called "the disastrous lapse in determinist logic."[4] Therefore, in vocation, as in so many other things, we're best served when we advance our stories in relationship with God. Love God, trust God, serve God, and listen to God. Then, choose. He won't wait at the end of the story as a reward for your success; He'll be with you all the while.

On the Mount of Olives the night He was betrayed, Jesus both yielded to God's will *and* chose to walk the road set before Him, and maybe we can likewise understand our role in shaping our stories. I think this is what Bob Goff was after when he said God wants us to do more than just bow our heads, but rather "bow our whole lives to Him instead."[5]

I once interviewed Erwin McManus for an article I was writing, and he pointed out the choices available to Adam and Eve in the garden. We tend to focus on God's single prohibition, "You must not eat from the tree of the knowledge of good and evil," forgetting the freedom that directly preceded it, "You are free to eat from any tree in the garden."[6] McManus told me that while we often think of God's will as a singular good choice among thousands of destructive options, the environment in which God created humanity was just the opposite. The garden was replete with all kinds of trees, and the man and woman were given the capacity to choose.[7]

> Without objective, there's no pursuit; without pursuit, there's no story.

Stories are made of choices, and it's this choice of an objective—*What do I want?*—that begins a story in earnest. Frodo doesn't leave the Shire and start toward Mount Doom without an objective. Rocky doesn't crack a raw egg into a glass and drink it without an objective. What about you? You might color inside the lines out of obligation, but you'll never create original art without an objective.

Gandhi said, "Action expresses priorities." Conversely, a lack of action expresses a lack of priorities (or priorities meaningful enough to elicit courage and conviction). Without objective, there's no pursuit; without pursuit, there's no story.

I'm not a naturally patient person, but when I am patient it's because a story has persuaded me to take a longer view of my circumstances. I'm not a naturally proactive man, but when I am proactive it's because a story has captured my heart and imagination. I'm not a naturally passionate fellow, but when I am passionate it's in service of a story about which I could not possibly remain dispassionate. This is how story moves me.

OUR STORY AS A JOURNEY WITH GOD

The point of invoking story in considering our objectives isn't to make life a consumer-driven exercise in naming and claiming your narrative of choice. Story is not an "If you can dream it, you can be it!" delivery mechanism. We can't scroll through the list of available lives and select the one that most appeals to our egos and our sensitive skin. If we could do that, the world would have plenty of rich, attractive, beloved celebrities but a tragic shortage of everything else. And then who would tend to the celebrities? See, the whole scenario breaks down in a hurry.

Rather, I hope our focus in story is a journey with God in which we discover where we're gifted, where we're needed, where we're challenged, and where we're loved. It's in these kinds of contexts, lives bowed, that we glimpse more and more of the people He created us to be.

Whatever objectives you land on as you attempt a life worthy of the calling you received, make sure you don't settle for something you're sure you can handle or attain on your own. Aim higher than that. Seek out something intimidating, risky, or borderline impossible. Dare to dream of stories in which you know that you couldn't possibly expect success of your own accord. As someone who is no stranger to anxiety and self-doubt, I understand if you're thinking, *Easy for you to say!* But believe me, the more you reflect on story and your life, the more you'll come to value audacity over circumstantial security.

The truth is great stories have high stakes. This is why so many novels, films, and TV shows involve police, lawyers, doctors, and soldiers—each occupation regularly deals with life and death, the highest of stakes. The uniforms mean the writers behind the stories can conjure drama in an instant, while a setting such as Dunder Mifflin, Inc., is much more conducive to comedy. When the writers of *The Office* want to tell a story, they must establish personal or professional stakes for the characters. Otherwise they're just telling jokes.

Whether or not you work for a regional paper and office supply company, you'll invariably find that small objectives make for small stakes, which make for small stories. As the old saying goes, "A ship in a harbour is safe, but that is not what ships are built for."[8] Small stories are manageable, but you and I were made for more.

WORK MATTERS

The apostle Paul covered several topics in his letter to the church at Ephesus, but I find it interesting that he repeatedly attaches spiritual stakes to work. In the first third of the letter, the stakes have to do with our identity and purpose. Paul tells his readers we are "God's handiwork, created in Christ Jesus to do good works, which God prepared in advance for us to do" (2:10). God worked with an objective in mind: that His workmanship would also work.

In the second third of the letter, Paul connects our work to communal stakes. Amid moral prescriptions for the "members of one body," he writes, "Anyone who has been stealing must steal no longer, but must work, doing something useful with their own hands, that they may have something to share with those in need" (4:25, 28). Suddenly, the lives of others are enjoined with our objectives. We must do something useful for the sake of the community.

In the final third of the letter, Paul increases the stakes by revealing who it is we're actually working for: "Slaves, obey your earthly masters with respect and fear, and with sincerity of heart, just as you would obey Christ. Obey them not only to win their favor when their eye is on you, but as slaves of Christ, doing the will of God from your heart. Serve wholeheartedly, as if you were serving the Lord, not people, because you know that the Lord will reward each one for whatever good they do, whether they are slave or free" (6:5–8).

There's much more to Ephesians than vocation and objective, but it's clear that God cares about these story lines within the broader narratives of our lives because of what's at stake. Work matters. We are His work, so we matter. Whatever we do, we can choose to do it in Him and to Him, for the benefit of the world around us.

GIVE YOUR ALL TO WHAT YOU MAKE

At the offices of W+K Dehli, an advertising agency in India, there is a large wall behind the reception area. On the wall, in a display that must stretch at least fifteen feet across, hundreds of yellow pencils protrude from the wall to spell out a simple maxim: "Work is worship."

As is perhaps befitting of the region, the saying originated with a 12th-century Indian guru named Basava.[9] I can only imagine how a people held down and dehumanized by the caste system might have responded to Basava's new story about the nature of work. The work of his followers was probably dirty, tedious, and exhausting—the opposite of what we associate with worshipful activities—so the "work is worship" idea represented dignity and liberation for the spirit as the body labored.

Most of us don't plow fields or shovel horse stalls, but we still have work to do. And work is still worship. "Whatever you do," Paul told the Colossians, "work at it with all your heart, as working for the Lord." We know that God ought to be the object of our worship—church has taught us that—but we're not so clear about work. Who is the object of our work? "It is the Lord Christ you are serving," Paul insists, and so we have our answer.[10]

We need not worry about sacred/secular distinctions. We need not worry about what we will eat or what we will wear. We need not fall in love with money, and we need not abstain from it. We need not compartmentalize our professional and spiritual lives. Instead, we need to remember who we're serving as we choose and pursue. Our stories have a way of revealing who we are, what we value, and who we worship.

So what do you want to make today? What do you want to make of the world? What do you want to do with what you've been given? What story are you going to tell? Don't look at me—I'm not an advisor anymore, although I suppose I could look at your transcripts if you'd like. Ultimately, these questions are asked of you, and you must answer.

Maybe you'll receive a clear and specific calling from on high. Or maybe you'll receive opportunities that require a combination of wisdom, discernment, and faith. In both scenarios, you'll still have choices to make: to step forward or stand pat, to give it your all or hold back.

The writer of Ecclesiastes knew life was short. "The Teacher" knew our stories spanned mere decades, not centuries or millennia, and thus he drew a conclusion about work: "Whatever your hand finds to do, do it with all your might" (9:10). In my experience, the best stories require all, not just a fraction, of a character's might. Wouldn't it be a shame to spend all we've got in the service of an unworthy objective? Or worse yet, what a tragedy it would be to save our might for a lifetime, always waiting in vain for a better objective to come along.

> We need to remember who we're serving as we choose and pursue. Our stories have a way of revealing who we are, what we value, and who we worship.

A great story is predicated on a worthy objective. If you haven't yet taken hold of a dream, desire, or cause to which you'd gladly give your life's work, perhaps it's time to make the pursuit of such an objective a priority.

Your story awaits.

conflict:
all is lost

"The best stories require all, not just a fraction, of a character's might. Wouldn't it be a shame to spend all we've got in the service of an unworthy objective?"

IN MY FRONT YARD YOU'LL find ants and worms. Once during a great summer drought the worms grew desperate—their skin, their soil, their very existence was shriveling and dying. In their distress, the worms began praying fervently to God for rain. The worms prayed and they waited, wondering if He cared or if He could hear them.

ANTS AND WORMS: A PARABLE

Meanwhile, the ants were thankful to God for His provision. They subsisted on water from the sprinkler system and seized upon creatures who fell victim to the summer sun. *God is good,* they told themselves, from friend to friend and parent to child. Unlike the weary worms, the ant community was thriving. The general tenor of their prayers was gratitude—God was clearly on their side and the ants wanted to keep it that way.

One day, the clouds gathered, the skies darkened, and it began to rain. The ants were wary. A little rain was good, but a lot of rain meant trouble for the supply lines and structures they'd built. When the rain strengthened into a full-blown Texas thunderstorm, the ants fled below ground to reinforce their hills and tunnels. The community's urgency gave way to terror as the colony began to take on water. *God,* the ants wondered, *where are You? What did we do to deserve this?*

The worms, meanwhile, were overjoyed. *Brothers and sisters, our prayers have been answered!* they proclaimed as they made their way to the surface. The abundant moisture reinvigorated the worms, and they reveled in their good fortune. They could trust God once again because He had delivered them from death, and so they decided to step out on faith and cross the great driveway in pursuit of more fertile pastures. Rather than crossing the Red Sea on dry land as the Israelites had done, the worms were spurred on by water covering what was normally a barren passage.

Below ground, the ants were in crisis. Their walls were crumbling, their food stores were spoiling, and their theology—formed in a season of abundance—was washed away. They worked to keep their heads above water, unable to shake their questions about what kind of deity would attempt to drown them in their homes with His aquatic fury. *Deliver us!* the ants cried.

The worms were almost halfway across the driveway when the rain stopped and the clouds gave way to an angry sun. Some of the worms turned back in hopes of reaching their old soil before the sun finished its work. The others pressed on, believing the rain would begin again or that God would otherwise guide them safely to new soil. Neither worm group reached its destination.

As the ants emerged from their soggy domiciles, they renewed their belief in a benevolent Creator. *Look, friends! The Lord has calmed the storm and now presents us with a bounty of fresh worms!* A chorus of amens and hallelujahs rose from the colony toward the sky.

The worms, marooned on a concrete killing field, knew their end was near. Their lives ebbed from their bodies and the darkness closed in. As the ants approached, the leader of the worms rasped, "What a cruel God we've got," and he exhaled for the last time. His body twisted awkwardly, and then he grew still.

A FALSE DILEMMA

I apologize for all the talk about ants and worms. That little exercise might have felt like something from the reject pile at Pixar, but I think it's a good way to frame this truth: our circumstances are an unreliable barometer for determining who God is and how He feels about us. The truth is we need something bigger than conflict to orient us in the world. We need a story that lends context to present struggles and hope to the resolution that awaits.

> As both Prince of Peace and Man of Sorrow, Jesus saw the world as bearing both the divine and the dysfunctional.

We're broken people in a broken world, and so our circumstances will break all to pieces from time to time. We only amplify our brokenness when we analyze the conflict in our lives and reach a self-pitying conclusion: God must either be evil, indifferent, or nonexistent. This is, of course, a false dilemma, a logical fallacy that considers only a few scraps of evidence and a handful of emotions.

It's a false dilemma because it excludes a reasonable alternative: both conflict and the love of God are inexorable parts of the human experience. The existence of one does not preclude the other. As both Prince of Peace and Man of Sorrows, Jesus saw the world as bearing both the divine and the dysfunctional. He walked the earth as God Incarnate, full of grace and truth, and yet he was despised, betrayed, and murdered.

"In this world you will have trouble," He told His followers. "But take heart! I have overcome the world."[1] This is not a platitude; it's a promise. It's a promise of both conflict and resolution, obstacle and victory, brokenness and wholeness. The dual guarantee of trouble and triumph is hope for us. It reveals the heart of a God who bestows sonship on wanton street urchins even though He knows we will quarrel, cuss, fib, and track mud on the antique rug. He knows we'll injure and be injured. But we're welcome because He knows the world and its brokenness has been overcome. This is part of the story.

AWFUL THINGS HAPPEN

My friend Michael was reflecting on our brokenness and the way it wreaks havoc on our stories when he remembered his grandfather's basement, which was full of audio and video equipment in various states of disrepair. "I now realize that he had the money to go out and buy the latest, fancy stuff," my friend wrote, "but he took pride in patching up and fixing the old broken things instead."[2]

> The storyteller encounters trouble and asks, "What's next?" because story is about pursuit.

Michael observed God is like that with our stories, assessing and repairing the brokenness and restoring us to the condition for which we were designed. God does not discard the broken things because He can still see a story in them. God actively pursues the healing of broken things in order that they might realize their stories in His story. I say all of this in hopes of communicating that some strands of undercooked theology ignore a reality that story assumes: conflict.

You will have trouble, Jesus said.

At our most self-involved and myopic, we encounter trouble and ask, "Why?!" because we want reasons. The storyteller, on the other hand, encounters trouble and asks, "What's next?" because story is about pursuit.

Let's say our objective was to escape a burning building. First, we try the door but find it blocked by a fallen beam and a curtain of flames. We can stop and scream at the heavens, demanding God give an account for this blazing lack of blessedness. Or we can accept the conflict and remember our objective. We can scan the room, locate a drawer of bedsheets, tie them together into a rope, fasten the rope to the dresser, and throw the rope out the open window. In reaching this specific objective, there is life. There's also a good story.

Remember Donald Miller's definition of story? A character who wants something and overcomes conflict to get it. This is exactly what we did in escaping the building—we wanted something and we overcame conflict to get it. Remove significant conflict from the equation and you get the kind of story that earns a "So what?" from its audience.

"My office building caught fire the other day."

"That must've been terrifying! Are you okay?"

"Well, it was at four a.m. on a Sunday, so the building was completely empty. No one was ever in danger, even for a minute. And in fact, the property damage only totaled a couple hundred dollars."

"Oh, okay. Anything else going on?"

"Wait, that wasn't a very good story, was it?"

"Terrible story. No doubt."

James Scott Bell says, "Without a character facing trouble that is understandable to the reader, you don't have a plot at all."[3] When Kurt Vonnegut compiled a list of advice for writing short stories, he put it this way: "Be a sadist. No matter how sweet and innocent your leading characters, make awful things happen to them—in order that the reader may see what they are made of."[4]

That's not to say God is a sadist by any means, but it speaks to how integral conflict is to story. We must know conflict is part of the deal. The question then is how we'll respond.

WHAT'S POSSIBLE?

I heard Ian Cron tell a story about being in the mountains with some friends. He shared with his friend Gail about conflict he was experiencing—a strained relationship with a family member. Looking thoughtfully at the mountains, Gail acknowledged the difficult situation. And then she asked a question Cron admits floored him:

> **"What does this make possible?"**
>
> **"I carry that question with me all the time now,"** Cron continued, as well we all should.[5] Gail's question is a great one because although it doesn't deny the conflict, the question refuses to despair in response to the conflict. The question frames conflict in an inherently hopeful story and wonders, "What's next?"

I think mountains were a fitting backdrop for Ian's conversation with Gail. There's a common type of mountains called fold mountains, which are formed when two tectonic plates collide. That's not the kind of conflict that just goes away, but it does make something possible: the layers of rock on top of the plates fold and climb upward, and a mountain is born. The conflict produces a new thing, and in many cases, a beautiful thing.

> The conflict produces a new thing, and in many cases, a beautiful thing.

Conflict makes story possible. Conflict sets the table for change. Conflict pushes characters out of comfort, familiarity, and ease. That's why Vonnegut told aspiring writers to make awful things happen to their characters. In our stories, sin makes redemption possible. Sickness makes healing possible. Brokenness makes restoration possible. Crucifixion makes resurrection possible.

Sure, we'd all prefer to forgo the conflict. We'd rather not have to ask ourselves, "What does this make possible?" But that isn't an option, and the sooner we let go of our delusional preference, the better off we'll be. We can either bemoan our circumstances and the fallen state of the cosmos, or we can make a decision about the kind of people we want to be. When the conflict hits—and it will hit—we won't return to our old tactics: the panic button, the bottle, the idol, the self-pity, the opposite sex. Instead we'll take a good look at the conflict, whatever it may be, and we'll start imagining the possibilities.

Blaine Hogan observed a similar proclivity toward imagination in Martin Scorsese's film *Hugo*. The child protagonist and his father are nearly done working on their robot when they discover a vital piece is missing. Hugo is crestfallen, knowing they're unlikely to find the missing piece. But his father whispers in what Blaine described as a wonderfully hopeful tone, "Ah, another mystery to solve!"[6]

Every time I read the father's words they stir my heart, probably because I'm still more prone to view the missing key with Hugo's dismay than with his father's adventurous hope. Even so, I've found that the father's words have given me something to pray these days, and I've taken great comfort from it.

Here's another mystery to solve, God, another story to tell. Help me see it that way. Teach me to trust. Teach me to follow. Help me see the story as it unfolds.

The more I think about it, the more I want the kind of faith and perspective that tempers what I'll call my Despair Reflex to the extent that I might immediately recognize the mystery and opportunity in conflict.

In his book *Drops Like Stars,* a meditation on the relationship between creativity and suffering, Rob Bell wrote, "Suffering can do that to us. We're jolted, kicked, prodded, and shoved into new realities we never would have brought about on our own. We're forced to imagine a new future because the one we were planning on is gone."[7] If you're like me, you read that quote and immediately thought of a time when your story, the future you were planning, seemed to fall apart. The good news is that while conflict is painful, it is not final.

> The good news is that while conflict is painful, it is not final.

We are a people of hope, redemption, and story. If we won't back down, and if the source of the conflict won't back down either, then perhaps we'll make a mountain.

CONFLICT AVOIDANCE

Some people revel in conflict, but I think most of us would rather avoid it—at least in our own lives. We would prefer to learn from our successes and other people's hardships. But sometimes even other people's conflict is too difficult to watch. My daughter often wants to skip straight to the third-act resolution on her *Veggie Tales* story CDs, and I understand where she's coming from. When I was a kid, I wanted my dad to erase the scene on our *Teen Wolf* VHS tape where Mick McAllister punches Scott Howard at the high school dance. I just wanted everyone to get along.

The presence of conflict paints an intense picture of the world, and the truth is that as an adult I still avert my eyes from time to time. I tell people I avoid the local news because of its ingrained inanity, and that's true, but I'm also not eager to hear about all the murder, theft, abuse, economic instability, and bureaucratic incompetence in my metropolitan area. When I'm bombarded with all that unresolved conflict, even the story about the precocious fifth-grader who took a basket of puppies to a retirement home can't cheer me up.

I avoid the local news because other people's conflict reminds me that the world is broken and that there are always obstacles between us and what we want. Other people's conflict reminds me just how fragile life is, and that message is too heavy for me before I go to bed. In the news and in my personal life, I'd rather avoid it. But I can't let conflict, or the possibility of pain, keep me from my story.

THAT HOT STOVE

We often talk about how pain can be a learning experience. If a child touches a hot stove and burns his hand, he learns not to touch the stove again. That's simple wisdom, right? But what would happen if children took the same lesson from every conflict? The first time they fell while trying to learn to walk would be the last time they ever let go of the coffee table. What if we let pain teach us to never again touch a bicycle or a musical instrument or a romantic relationship? What if we let trauma keep us from developing passions and skills and experiencing life to its fullest?

The stove lesson works for the stove, but it isn't a one-size-fits-all response to hardship. We can't learn to interpret the slightest hint of conflict—pain, suffering, setbacks, resistance—as a message from God or common sense telling us to stop and turn around. If we want to tell great stories—or have a great story to tell—we have to understand the difference between stove pain and bicycle pain. Of course stove pain signals us to stay away—there is no benefit that awaits us beyond the recklessness of touching searing metal. But bicycle pain is different. If we're willing to endure the fear, anxiety, wobbliness, and scrapes, a whole new world will open up to us. Learning to ride a bike is, as I recall, pure conflict. But for those who push through, the ability to ride is pure possibility.

MOVE YOUR FEET

The other night I was telling my wife about a situation that was taking its toll on me. I was frustrated by what happened and the thought of slogging through the conflict in search of some sort of resolution was exhausting. I emitted a long sigh, as I'm prone to do when I'm feeling both dramatic and listless.

"Everything will work out," Annie said—a quick nod to Romans 8:28. She paused and I started to feel better. Then, as though she could sense my tendency toward passivity and avoidance, she added, "But everything won't just go away. You're going to have to *do* something."

I didn't feel better anymore because she was right. Resolution wasn't going to just happen to me while I scoured Netflix for something *(anything)* worth streaming. Resolution was waiting for me to start walking, to dig for it, to do the work. If resolution was my objective, I was going to have to endure conflict to reach it. I wasn't waiting for resolution; resolution was waiting for me.

I believe this is true in most conflict/resolution dynamics—we can't be mere recipients of resolution; we have to be participants in it. The depth and breadth of our participation will vary from context to context—you know that—but the persistent truth is that resolution will not be bestowed upon us while we're sleeping like a dollar from the tooth fairy. Unless, of course, you only have problems like, "My leg hurt last night, but when I woke up this morning it felt fine." In that case, I guess resolution did come when you were sleeping. But if that's you, well, you need to get some more interesting problems.

Like I said, Annie was right. She usually is. As much as I didn't want to, I had to work through this particular conflict and help move things toward resolution. I thought carefully about what happened, I prayed for wisdom and healing, and then I participated in the resolution process. It wasn't easy, but easy isn't much of an objective. An African proverb goes something like, "Pray, but when you pray, move your feet." I think that's what story and conflict require of us—an intentional movement of the feet. It reminds me of the first words Jesus offered His disciples: "Follow me."

THE CONTRIBUTION OF WRONGS

So what do we *do* with conflict? The answer, at least as far as this book is concerned, is we must frame it in story. As we've established, story says conflict is to be expected. But story is not pessimistic or nihilistic—just the opposite! Story also says that conflict is not all; conflict is not the end. Story, in general, is about pursuit and encompasses past, present, and future. The Christian story in particular identifies Jesus as our past, present, and future, and so our pursuit is endowed with hope in the context of relationship.

Through the lens of story, we're empowered to acknowledge that conflict tests us, shapes us, and changes the way we see the world—ourselves, our objectives, and our neighbors. Conflict, properly framed, imbues us with perspective. We can count the cost of that which we pursue. We can assess the triviality of our worries and comforts. We can empathize with others who have been wounded on the journey.

Conflict can yield both good stories and good storytellers. Overcoming conflict and integrating it into our stories gives us an entry point into connecting with others in our weakness. Conflict helps us become His witnesses—we identify with Christ in His suffering and we experience a measure of the bad news which necessitates good news.

In *The End of Memory: Remembering Rightly in a Violent World*, theologian Miroslav Volf reflects at length upon a year he spent in the Yugoslavian military, during which he was the subject of systematic surveillance, manipulation, and interrogation. In the book,

Volf considers what we can and should make of what he calls "wrongs suffered." At the heart of one of his conclusions is story.

"We integrate [wrongs suffered] into our life-story by coming to understand how they contribute to the goodness of the whole. We perceive that, in one way or another, they have made us better people."[8] In other words, we give a conflict a place. We take a difficult situation—in Volf's case, a difficult *year*—and we refuse to view it in isolation. Rather we view conflict as a scene, a chapter, in a story that spans a lifetime and beyond.

Volf also exhorts us to look beyond our own stories at the broader scope of history. Specifically, he identifies the Exodus story and the Passion story as "the two central events of redemptive history" and he labels them "sacred memories."[9] By engaging these sacred memories in their context we encounter the opportunity to discover who we are as the people of God, an enduring hope for the future, and the heart of the Redeemer.

Volf writes:

> We remember, and looking at the past we see the future. If the Exodus is our story, then we remember deliverance not only as the past deliverance of our community, but also as our and our community's future deliverance. The story of the Exodus tells not just what happened "then and there": but also what will happen in our own future. Similarly, if Christ's story is our story, then in remembering Christ we remember not just his past but also in a significant sense our future.[10]

When we meet conflict head-on, sacred memories root us in the God who has rescued, redeemed, and sustained His beloved ones for thousands of years.

Joseph—he of the Technicolor dream coat—was forced to confront the wrongs he suffered as a result of his brothers' treachery when they appeared before him years later. But by that time, Joseph had framed the conflict he endured in the larger context of his life story. He was a wise ruler now, no longer a careless boy, and he knew that his hardships had not been the end of him. On the contrary, his journey shaped him into the man he'd become. Joseph's brothers threw themselves at his feet, desperate for mercy instead of vengeance. "Don't be afraid," he assured them. "You intended to harm me, but God intended it for good to accomplish what is now being done, the saving of many lives."[11]

> We tell the stories we find ourselves in, even when we're waist-deep in conflict.

Joseph didn't deny, minimize, or repress his suffering—he integrated it into his story. When Joseph looked at his story he found God there, doing the things we know God does—making good from evil, shining light in darkness, and causing hope to spring forth from ashes.

If we acknowledge that conflict is inevitable, and if we participate in the practice of viewing conflict in the context of narrative, what then? We must persist in telling our stories. Our objectives, whatever they may be, still need pursuing. And our calling as witnesses to His story still needs fulfilling.

The challenge, as Annie and I found out during our adoption process, is that it's difficult to tell your story while you're still in the middle of it. Telling your story in the midst of unresolved struggles—doubts, anxiety, and pain—requires a certain amount of conviction. Why? Because you can't be entirely sure there will be a happy ending, or at the very least, you can't be sure what form the happy ending will take. A seasoned trial attorney will never ask a question she doesn't already know the answer to, but committed storytellers don't always have the same luxury. We tell the stories we find ourselves in, even when we're waist-deep in conflict.

FACING YOUR GIANTS

As storytellers we'll always be tempted by tidy narratives— stories with minimal conflict and maximum resolution. Our understanding of faith might even push us toward stories in which every source of conflict is eventually met with overwhelming good fortune.

In *Facing the Giants,* Coach Grant Taylor has three major problems: his football team stinks, money is tight, and his wife can't seem to get pregnant. Then the coach has a spiritual epiphany. As a result, he's a better coach, a better man, and a better husband. In the end (SPOILER ALERT), the coach succeeds in every area of his life. Not only has Coach Taylor grown spiritually, all the problems he had in act 1 are eradicated by act 3.

When a screenwriter offers us a script, he or she is generally offering us a statement about life. And while I don't want to be overly critical of *Facing the Giants,* I find its statement about life to be attractive but inaccurate. A burgeoning relationship with God is absolutely to our benefit as human beings, but such a relationship is not the catalyst for a systemic elimination of the conflict in our lives. Faith in and obedience to God are what's best for us, but they're not meant to be associated with us getting everything we want.

Sure, your team might win state. Or as some high school football coaches will tell you, your team might get taken behind the woodshed each and every Friday night this season. Your cash flow situation might improve and you might get a new truck—perhaps it will have a Hemi. Or as millions of Americans will tell you, you might have to keep pouring oil and coolant into the old jalopy for another year. Your wife might finally get pregnant after months or years of trying. Or as some of my family's dearest friends will tell you, you might have to make some adjustments to your picture of what a family looks like.

SCARS OF HURT . . . AND HEALING

Scenarios like these play out every day. Our perception of our stories and our understanding of conflict can either help us trust God with our circumstances *or* shape us into entitled victims who interpret any prolonged difficulty as a broken promise from a God we trusted to deliver the goods. I don't mean to sound harsh, but the truth is that I've been there. I've seen it plenty in myself and others, but I've never seen it end well. The stories that do end well, however, are stories characterized by perseverance, faithfulness, patience, and selflessness.

If we're honest, if we're telling the truth, conflict will be apparent in our stories. Church culture and our pride may both encourage us to downplay conflict in our stories, but we must resist. "There cannot be any 'story' without a fall—all stories are ultimately about the fall," Tolkein wrote.[12] So while our scars shouldn't become the centerpiece of our identity, neither should we hide them.

> Church culture and our pride may both encourage us to downplay conflict in our stories, but we must resist.

In fact, scars present us with an interesting choice to make in regard to conflict and story. We can point to our scars and tell a sad story—after all, scars are evidence that we've been hurt. If we're so inclined, each scar can be a testimony to injustice and the indifference of God. Or, and this is a big or, we can tell a more redemptive tale. We can rightly interpret scars as evidence of both hurt and healing. I don't say this lightly because I know some wounds run deeper than I can imagine. But God is in the business of turning wounds into scars. Church culture and our pride may both encourage us to downplay conflict in our stories, but we must resist.

There's a story behind every scar, and our scars can be altars that call us to remember God's faithfulness. They can be signposts that point others to His faithfulness for the first time because we are witnesses. That's the story our scars can tell—that's how conflict figures into all of this—if we're willing to give voice to them. Henri Nouwen said that just as Jesus made "his own broken body the way to health, to liberation and new life," so we also are called "to make [our] wounds into a major source of [our] healing power."[13] Nouwen's idea of the wounded healer is a vision for where conflict fits within our stories—it's where the wounds of the past meet ministry in the present and redemption in the future.

BOASTING IN CONFLICT

In 2 Corinthians 12:7–10, Paul tells the story of one particular struggle with conflict. He was tormented by what he called, "a thorn in [his] flesh, a messenger from Satan." Whatever form this specific conflict took, Paul desperately asked God to take it away, just as any of us would. What I find so interesting is the response Paul received: "But He said to me, 'My grace is sufficient for you, for my power is made perfect in weakness.'" In God's response we see that He prefers to walk with us through stories that include conflict, as opposed to transporting us from a difficult story to something more paradisiacal.

Rather than *take*, God promised Paul He would *give*—His grace, Himself. God's promise was that what He gave would be enough. While I frequently follow Paul's lead in begging God to remove the conflict in my life, I rarely follow his lead in embracing God's promise of grace amid conflict: "Therefore I will boast all the more gladly about my weaknesses, so that Christ's power may rest on me."

Even at my most humble and self-effacing, I'm reticent to share personal stories like the one Paul told the Corinthians. And yet as Paul taught the Corinthians in his first letter to them, "God chose the foolish things of the world to shame the wise."[14] When

Paul happily recalled the story of his weakness, he was recogniz-
ing how his small story fit into God's massive story. After all, Paul
was an apostle of Jesus—the One in whom all things were made
and the One who made Himself nothing. In Jesus we have the
story of the Son of God putting on flesh, becoming obedient to
death, and rising again in a body that bore the scars of His murder. When Thomas refused to believe the resurrection until he saw
the evidence for himself, Jesus could have responded with a show
of power, a flashy miracle that reestablished the deity-humanity
chasm between Him and His mates. Instead, He offered Thomas
the proof he demanded: the wounds. "Put your finger here; see my
hands," Jesus said. "Reach out your hand and put it into my side.
Stop doubting and believe."[15]

As we know, behind those scars lies quite a story.

KEEP GOING

You have some objectives: to follow Christ, to bear witness
to His story, to love your family, to serve your neighbors, to go to
college, to start a business, to contribute to the flourishing of your
community, and so on. As your story unfolds and you pursue these
objectives, you will endure conflict. What then? Will you stop?

Story says no. Like Peter and John before the Sanhedrin (Acts
4), story says *we cannot stop*. So, if your objective is worth it, keep
going. Tell your story.

purpose: beyond the macguffin

"Let the redeemed of the Lord tell their story."

I'VE MADE A LOT OF mistakes in my life. More specifically, I've made a lot of mistakes related to food. Once when I was in college I found myself in Chattanooga, Tennessee, with some friends on a crisp fall afternoon. Bryan and his wife, Amy, who lived in Chattanooga at the time, took me and a guy named Derrick to a burger joint that just so happened to be celebrating its grand opening that weekend.

THE GREAT CHEESEBURGER INCIDENT

Our server explained that we could choose from five different sizes of cheeseburger: 5.5 ounces, 7 ounces, 10 ounces, 14 ounces, and 20 (yes, 20) ounces. Then she said that whoever actually consumes the 20-ounce cheeseburger in its entirety gets his or her (let's face it: mostly his) picture on the wall. The wall of fame.

The four of us looked over at the wall and, being that this was opening weekend, found it empty. Derrick and I looked at each other and thought, We could be the first pictures on the wall at a cheeseburger shack in Chattanooga, Tennessee. We knew what we had to do—Derrick and I both opted for the 20-ounce monstrosity.

Let me be clear: ordering that cheeseburger was a mistake. I know that now.

I should have stopped eating somewhere around ounce 11. My body's signals were calm but clear: No need for any more ground meat, big guy. We're all full down here. I looked at the plate and the blank wall of fame and at Derrick. We knew what we had to do—Derrick and I both kept eating until we'd finished our cheeseburgers. Listen, finishing that cheeseburger was a mistake. I know that now.

When the server returned from the kitchen with the Polaroid camera and a look of pity on her face, we couldn't even smile as she snapped our photos for the wall. My body's signals took on a decidedly worried tone: What did you do? Why did you do it? How are we going to make this right? Better yet, how are we going to survive?

Unfortunately, I didn't have any answers for my body; I only had bad news. We weren't driving from the restaurant to a nice soft couch or a welcoming emergency room. No, we were driving to the airport so that Derrick and I could fly back to Dallas. (Gulp.)

Over the course of my life, through some combination of divine intervention, grace, good fortune, and random chance, I've made a lot of mistakes while largely avoiding the worst possible consequences of those mistakes. There have still been consequences, but the fallout has rarely been as bad as it could have been. Let me be clear one last time: the Great Cheeseburger Incident of 2000 was a situation in which I probably did experience the worst possible consequences of a mistake. I know that now. If only I'd known it when I was placing my order that fateful day. Instead, a gigantic cheeseburger figures prominently into the lessons I learned in college that weren't on a syllabus.

THE LESSON

To me, the most important part of the cheeseburger story is what happened the next morning. It was a Monday and I had class, so after my alarm went off I shuffled over to the cafeteria. I got some food, sat down, and ate breakfast. Just eighteen hours after the most calorie-intensive, protein-packed, gut-ballooning meal of my entire life, I was hungry again. So I ate.

Call me crazy, but that means something. And not just that I had the overactive metabolism of an eighteen-year-old (which I did). It means that our bodies are never content for long. No matter how much you eat and how satisfied you feel, you'll get hungry again. No matter how much water you drink, you'll get thirsty again. No matter how much sleep you get in a given night, you'll get tired again. Our bodies are incapable of sustained satisfaction. But it doesn't stop there, does it?

You could experience a perfect day of companionship with your spouse or best friend, but after a few days of

> This state of temporary satisfaction is something we all live with...at the very least this reality constantly propels us forward in our stories.

isolation your hunger for interpersonal connection would return. You could get on a roll at work and have the best quarter in the history of your organization, but after a week or two of busywork your yearning for professional fulfillment would be gnawing at you again.

You haven't won the game of life when you've managed to sate all your desires at the same time. All you've done is performed routine self-maintenance—you've kept your heart, mind, and body from reaching 0 percent like a laptop battery on a cross-country flight. Given enough time, you'll need more food, water, sleep, money, conversation, prayer, connection, love, sex, etc. In other words, we can't sit still for too long or we'll die. However good it was, we have to keep moving. We have to keep going forward because it won't be long before we need something else.

What I'm trying to get at in all of this is that this state of temporary satisfaction is something we all live with, and although this might reek of the fall, at the very least this reality constantly propels us forward in our stories, even if we have no idea that's what is happening. The fact that we're always churning with needs and desires means that one objective or another—however epic or insignificant—is always before us and we're always in pursuit. Whether we chase that which helps us thrive or settle for whatever will enable us to survive for another day is up to us.

We play many parts in our lives. We are children, siblings, parents, spouses, friends, neighbors, students, and professionals. We're ascribed several roles in the Bible. We are saints, disciples, priests, servants, ambassadors, followers of the Way. But there's one role that might pull all these other distinctions together: the role of witness.

You are meant to be a storyteller.

DRIVEN TO STORIES

Bruce Springsteen once told *Rolling Stone*, "All artists are psychologically and emotionally driven to tell their stories."[1] I'm not one to disagree with the Boss—mostly because millions of people call him the Boss—but I wonder if his statement stops short. It's not only artists who are driven to tell their stories; it's everyone. Is there a human being who isn't compelled to share who they are, where they've been, and where they dream of going? We're all driven to tell our stories; artists are just the ones who scream their stories into a microphone while wearing leather pants . . . or whose stories include hobbits and aliens and sultry vampires. But everyone tells stories, and conveniently enough, everyone is drawn to stories.

As a Christian I believe we were made to tell and respond to stories. In a world of divergent narratives, God calls us to tell His story. A conversation between Jesus and His disciples found in Acts 1 explores this calling. The conversation takes place after Jesus' death and resurrection, and the lads have a question for Him: "Lord, are you at this time going to restore the kingdom to Israel?" (v. 6)

It's a fair question. They'd been through a lot—the agony of losing Jesus and the joy of regaining Him—but at the heart of the question is the hope that Jesus would get to work changing the world. Now that they'd suffered a little bit, they were hoping it was over and that Jesus would set things right. What they didn't realize is that they had it backwards—He intended for them to get to work changing the world. Restoring the kingdom to Israel would have meant the overthrow of the Roman bureaucrats and soldiers who carried out the crucifixion. A restored kingdom, featuring Jesus as the benevolent king, also would have meant an end to the religious tyranny of the Pharisees, so it's no wonder the disciples were eager to know if the time had come. But as is often the case with our earnest questions, Jesus had something different in mind.

> God had a plan, and the people who followed Jesus were right in the thick of it.

"You will receive power when the Holy Spirit comes on you," Jesus tells them, "and you will be my witnesses in Jerusalem, and in all Judea and Samaria, and to the ends of the earth"(v. 8).

The disciples had work to do, and that work was to be witnesses. God had a plan, and the people who followed Jesus were right in the thick of it. Simply put, witnesses experience a sequence of events (a story unfolding), and then they tell that story. Jesus could have labeled His followers soldiers, entrepreneurs, watchdogs, or a number of other things, but He chose witnesses because He knew His story would change the world. And with that message delivered, with that role and purpose established, Jesus had nothing more to say. "After he said this, he was taken up before their very eyes, and a cloud hid him from their sight" (v. 9). With this sequence of events, Jesus set the gold standard for the word "delegate."

Just one chapter later, in Acts 2, the early believers were filled with the Holy Spirit on the day of Pentecost. When the crowds start to wonder what has gotten into the Spirit-filled believers, Peter embraces his newfound charge to be a witness by delivering a powerful sermon. He begins by quoting the prophet Joel, and then he bears witness to the story of Christ:

> **"Jesus of Nazareth was a man accredited by God to you by miracles, wonders and signs, which God did among you through him, as you yourselves know. This man was handed over to you by God's deliberate plan and foreknowledge; and you, with the help of wicked men, put him to death by nailing him to the cross. But God raised him from the dead, freeing him from the agony of death, because it was impossible for death to keep its hold on him."** (vv. 22–24)

Peter then circles back to Israel's story by quoting David in Psalm 16, establishing Jesus as the continuation and culmination of God's plan for His people. When some in the audience ask Peter how they should respond to this revelation, he offers them a new story going forward: "Repent and be baptized, every one of you, in the name of Jesus Christ for the forgiveness of your sins. And you will receive the gift of the Holy Spirit. The promise is for you and your children and for all who are far off—for all whom the Lord our God will call" (vv. 38–39).

Luke estimates that about three thousand people heeded Peter's call to repent of their sins and be baptized as new followers of Christ. If there were any doubts about why Jesus told His friends they would be His witnesses—or what exactly He meant by that label—I imagine those doubts didn't survive Pentecost. Rather, at that point, their purpose must have been reasonably clear: experience the story, then be a witness to it. In the next two chapters of Acts, Peter and John do just that.

"WE CAN'T KEEP QUIET"

Beginning in Acts 3:1, Peter and John were headed to the temple one afternoon when a beggar who was lame asked them for money. I imagine Peter was like me—he never carried cash. So Peter looked at the man and said, "Silver or gold I do not have but what I do have, I give you. In the name of Jesus Christ of Nazareth, walk." Peter and John help him up, and the guy can walk. The text says he was "walking and jumping and praising God." The crowd recognizes the formerly lame man, and they're amazed. Peter, still attuned to his calling to be a witness, takes the opportunity to tell the crowd a story:

> "Fellow Israelites, why does this surprise you? Why do you stare at us as if by our own power or godliness we had made this man walk? The God of Abraham, Isaac and Jacob, the God of our fathers, has glorified his servant Jesus. You handed him over to be killed, and you disowned him before Pilate, though he had decided to let him go. You disowned the Holy and Righteous One and asked that a murderer be released to you. You killed the author of life, but God raised him from the dead. We are witnesses of this. By faith in the name of Jesus, this man whom you see and know was made strong. It is Jesus'

name and the faith that comes through him that has completely healed him, as you can all see." (vv. 12–16)

If you've read any Scripture passages about the priests and
other religious authorities during this time, you might guess they
did not like the story Peter and John were telling. The religious
rulers summoned Peter and John and asked, "By what power or
what name did you do this?" Once again, Peter was ready to tell
them a story:

> "Rulers and elders of the people! If we are being called
> to account today for an act of kindness shown to a man
> who was lame and are being asked how he was healed,
> then know this, you and all the people of Israel: It is by
> the name of Jesus Christ of Nazareth, whom you cruci-
> fied but whom God raised from the dead, that this man
> stands before you healed. Jesus is 'the stone you builders
> rejected, which has become the cornerstone.' Salvation is
> found in no one else, for there is no other name under
> heaven given to mankind by which we must be saved."
> (Acts 4:8–12)

The rulers were astonished, and they were also trapped because the healed man was standing right there. They couldn't pun-
ish or discredit the disciples in front of the gobsmacked crowd,
so they dismissed Peter and John that they might talk amongst
themselves. The best strategy the religious could come up with was
to call Peter and John back and command them to stop speaking
and teaching in the name of Jesus. It's to this command that Peter
and John offer an essential response. "But Peter and John replied,
'Which is right in God's eyes: to listen to you, or to him? You be
the judges! As for us, we cannot help speaking about what we have
seen and heard'" (vv. 19–20).

That's it, right there: "we cannot help speaking about what we have seen and heard." A few translations say, "we can't stop . . ." and I love the way *The Message* paraphrases it: "As for us, there's no question—we can't keep quiet about what we've seen and heard."

This is what it means to be a storyteller in the kingdom of God. This is what it means when Jesus says, "You will be My witnesses." The Greek word used is *martys,* meaning someone who offers a testimony. If you think about it, Peter and John's phrase— "what we've seen and heard"—fits with what we ask of a witness in our legal system: "What did you see? What did you hear?" Everything else is hearsay.

> "We cannot help speaking about what we have seen and heard."

Peter and John demonstrate that this kind of storytelling is what God asks of us when they contrast listening to the religious rulers ("stop speaking") or listening to God ("you will be My witnesses"). In their example, in their faithfulness, in their understanding of who God was calling them to be, we find a foundation for what it means to serve God, the church, and the world through story.

Going back to my disagreement with Mr. Springsteen, we're all driven to tell our stories. But followers of Christ are compelled to tell *His* story. This is not a job or a prerequisite for getting into heaven—it's who we are. We *see* Him working in the world, we *hear* His voice, we tell those stories. As He said, we will be His witnesses.

THE PRICE OF WITNESS

Early on in my process of writing this book, renowned war correspondent Marie Colvin and photographer Rémi Ochlik were killed while covering the dangerous conflict in Syria. A *New York Magazine* piece published in the wake of Colvin and Ochlik's deaths was titled, "The Risks of Bearing Witness: Discussing Marie Colvin's Legacy."[2]

Marie Colvin's life and death have tremendous implications for us. As the article suggests, storytellers are not surrounded by a force field of good intentions. In fact, at times the commitment to observe, live, and tell meaningful stories will put us in harm's way. Colvin and Ochlik paid the ultimate price, as did celebrated photojournalist Tim Hetherington in Libya in 2011. Dan Woolley traveled to Haiti in January 2010 as part of a team filming in Port-au-Prince for Compassion International when the massive earthquake struck. Woolley survived, buried in the rubble of his hotel for sixty-five hours awaiting rescue, all the while suffering from a compound fracture in his leg and other injuries. Woolley's colleague David Hames did not survive the earthquake.

Most of us will never find ourselves taking shelter from mortar shells or clinging to life in a developing country ravaged by a natural disaster, but being a witness comes with a price. To the prideful and powerful, the gospel story will always be threatening. If the gospel were convenient or self-evident, our calling would not be so urgent. Instead, we have to bear witness in the midst of indifference, hostility, and, yes, danger.

THE STORY FROM THE INSIDE

Psalm 107 is this beautiful exploration of the way God rescues people from their distress, and it begins with this instruction: "Let the redeemed of the Lord tell their story" (v. 2). Like Jesus' declaration that His followers would be His witnesses, this command from the Psalms requires us to find our voices and use them to tell stories. And both this phrase from Psalm 107 ("their story") and Peter and John's words from Acts 4 ("what we've seen and heard") connect us as storytellers to the story itself.

This is an important distinction. We tell the story from the inside, as participants in it. We're witnesses, not gossip junkies passing along a rumor we've heard. Sure, the story preceded us, but it didn't stop there. We're caught up in it, this rabbit hole of a gospel we've tumbled down. Storytellers share the life and truth in themselves in hopes that the life and truth might take hold in others.

Frederick Buechner wrote, "The task of the preacher is to hold up life to us; by whatever gifts he or she has of imagination, eloquence, simple candor, to create images of life through which we can somehow see into the wordless truth of our lives."[3] He was writing to preachers, but don't let that scare you. A preacher is just someone who has been called to do for a living what we're all called to do with our lives—be a storyteller; be a witness. I'm no preacher, but Buechner was talking to me. I think he was talking to you, too.

TRUE STORIES MATTER

My family's adoption journey ran the gamut of human emotions. We experienced what Homer Simpson once described as "the terrifying lows, the dizzying highs, the creamy middles!" Through it all, we told our story. We couldn't help but speak (or blog) about what we'd seen and heard in the process. We weren't experienced, skilled, articulate, or particularly strategic; we were just witnesses.

> There is something at stake in our stories.

I can tell you without hesitation that I've never felt more alive than when Annie and I lived and told the story to which God led us. I wasn't thinking about Acts 1:8 and Acts 4:20 at the time, and I didn't know that my purpose or calling in life was to be a storyteller. But looking back, it's plain to me why I felt so alive and why our roller coaster adoption affected so many people: because true stories matter.

I'd be lying if I said I understood most of what's going on in Revelation, but there's a fascinating sequence in chapter 12 you should know about. A cosmic war breaks out between the good guys (Michael and his angels) and the bad guys (the dragon and his angels). When the dragon is defeated, a loud voice from heaven provides some narration:

> Now have come the salvation and the power
> and the kingdom of our God,
> and the authority of his Messiah.
> For the accuser of our brothers and sisters,
> who accuses them before our God day and night,
> has been hurled down. (v. 10)

Amid the poetry of the passage, we get a glimpse of the implications of the war. God and His Messiah have cast down our accuser. The very next passage has something to say about the cosmic importance that bearing witness has in this conflict:

> They triumphed over him
> by the blood of the Lamb
> *and by the word of their testimony;*
> they did not love their lives so much
> as to shrink from death. (v. 11 emphasis mine)

Permit me to reiterate that I'm not an end-times guru or even a proper biblical scholar. But when I read that our accuser is overcome by some formidable combination of the blood of Christ and true stories about His redemptive work, I know it means something. It means, throughout the Bible, the people of God are called on to be storytellers as they follow Him. It means there is something at stake in our stories.

It means we were made for this.

the storyteller, culture, and people

"The people of God are called on to be storytellers as we follow Him."

EACH OF US IS AN inhabitant of culture, and we're each shaped by whatever culture we inhabit. And just as narrative is an important force within our individual lives, so also is narrative an important force within culture. Let's briefly explore, then, how we as storytellers might understand our relationship to culture and our relationship to our fellow inhabitants.

STORY AND CULTURE

Culture is, in some way, a collection of shared values and the communal expression of what we value. James Davison Hunter describes it as "a system of truth claims and moral obligations."[1] Combined with Andy Crouch's assertion that culture is what we make of the world,[2] I tend to understand culture as the inward beliefs and outward practices that make a stranger feel like a stranger when she visits a foreign land.

However, that's not to say a culture is necessarily homogeneous from top to bottom. For example, under the wide umbrella of present-day American culture we find a spectrum of ethnicities, religious creeds and dispositions, political predilections, and so on. In the broadest of terms, we can group these apparently disparate peoples into the same culture because of what they share: a connection to the American narrative, however vague that narrative might be.

What does that mean exactly? I think it means that regardless of heritage or hermeneutic, the American culture comprises those who are affected—physically, psychologically, emotionally, financially, spiritually, morally—by common stimuli: presidential elections, military conflicts, economic meltdowns, existential crises, artistic movements, entertainment trends, fashion revolutions, technological advancements, and, of course, whatever personalities are currently trending. You might hop into a New York City cab driven by a man from whom you appear to be hopelessly different, but if both of you are shaped by September 11th, gonzo journalism, the health care debate, Twitter, and reality TV, well, you're part of the same culture.

The connection between culture and story, then, is that within a given culture there exists a kind of story exchange. About culture Hunter also observes, "[truth claims and moral demands] are embedded within narratives that often have overlapping themes and within various myths that often reinforce common ideals."[3] Practically speaking, this story exchange can only happen in a context where participants share enough language, symbols, and mores to communicate intelligibly with one another, which is why unique geographies and histories give rise to unique cultures. It's within these unique cultures that the church has always found herself awash in the tension of competing narratives.

CHURCH AND CULTURE

For as long as the people of God have been primarily concerned with His kingdom while the culture at-large has been primarily concerned with other pursuits, an antagonistic relationship has existed between the two entities. This trend is as evident in the book of Acts as it is in the current rhetoric surrounding the issues we refer to as the "traditional view of marriage" or the "sanctity of life."

For people of faith, it's difficult to watch as our culture gives rise to secularism and all manner of other "-isms" that are an affront to our sacred beliefs. It's enough to make us revile culture, to shudder and squirm beneath its broken blanket, and imagine what it would be like to escape from the tide-pool-turned-cesspool that is our modern milieu, and instead take up residence in an exclusive community of right belief.

To be honest, this impulse is one of the factors that attracted me, as a graduating senior at a public high school, to the idea of a Christian college. I thought life would be a lot more edifying and a lot less convoluted, and it almost was. The college was a city (okay, a small village) on a literal hill replete with prayer in classes, mandatory worship services, rules and regulations for student behavior, curfew, and a big fence. And yet I didn't get my escapist wish because, as it turns out, I smuggled the convolution in with me. As Jesus said,

> The Romans spread Greek throughout the empire; the apostles made it the *lingua franca* of the early church.

"What comes out of a person is what defiles them. For it is from within, out of a person's heart, that evil thoughts come—sexual immorality, theft, murder, adultery, greed, malice, deceit, lewdness, envy, slander, arrogance and folly. All these evils come from inside and defile a person."[4]

I don't mean to critique my alma mater or any other Christian college. Rather, my target is the urge I once harbored to avoid culture. In the years since I graduated from college, I've come to see how ducking culture was my way of ducking my calling to bear witness to the story of God to the people He loves. Thank God the apostles weren't as apt to sidestep the gospel as I was. After all, they'd walked in the footsteps of Jesus, and just as He embedded Himself with humanity through the incarnation, so the apostles embedded themselves within the cultures of the ancient Near East. The tension between the church and the culture was there, but the apostles lived in the tension and operated under it.

The Romans built and protected the roads; the apostles traveled down them. The Romans spread Greek throughout the empire; the apostles made it the *lingua franca* of the early church. In some sense, the apostles were architects of a new culture within a culture, but pagans were the architects of the macro-culture into which the church was born. The first leaders of the church seemingly accepted this tension. In response, they told a story in the macro-culture that invited people into a sacred community.

I'm hardly the first to turn to Acts 17, the story of the apostle Paul at Mars Hill, in a conversation about engaging culture, and with good reason. As Paul walked through ancient Athens, Luke records he was "greatly distressed to see that the city was full of idols" (v. 16). And yet, even in his distress, Paul didn't flee. Rather, he "looked carefully at [their] objects of worship"(v. 23). From Paul's study of Athenian idols he extrapolated some measure of the Athenian story. Again, he didn't flee. For Paul, a committed witness, the parade of idols was an invitation to tell a story, not an indication that he should leave in search of a municipality that wasn't so pagan. When Paul reached the meeting of the Areopagus, he stood before the gathered elites and told them a story about God, humanity, relationship, justice, and the resurrection of Jesus.

Some sneered, some questioned, and some believed. As for Paul, he eventually left Athens for Corinth, but only *after* he'd been a witness to the people there.

THE GAME

The last thing I want to do is become the thousandth middle-class white guy to offer his cultural analysis of David Simon's acclaimed HBO series *The Wire*, so I'll steer clear of extracting any social theories from a television show. I don't know anything about race, politics, socioeconomic conditions, criminal justice, or crack cocaine, but as I watched the show I saw one principle at work over and over again. It's something I heard Tim Keller say a time or two via his sermon's podcast: people's beliefs about the future shape the choices they make in the present. In other words, the stories we tell ourselves about where our lives are headed directly influence how we live.

In *The Wire*, a Baltimore housing project offers its residents a bleak story. It's a story with a future but no hope—only poverty, violence, abuse, drugs, decay, and marginalization. The story is so utterly convincing to most of the characters on *The Wire* that they surrender to it in one way or another. The show's central focus within the city of Baltimore was "the game"—the world of drug kingpins, pushers, and users. The story of the projects was so bad that a generation of young men chose the game, a despicable story of slinging crack and dodging bullets. Choosing the game meant choosing an early grave or a life spent in and out of prison, but the boys who chose the game didn't care. Why? Because the stories of both the players in the game *and* the residents on the sidelines had an inevitability to them. Both were lives of struggle that sooner or later ended in death. The young men chose the game because it afforded them a temporary modicum of empowerment, provision, and community, and it didn't matter that the story ended in a chalk outline or an orange jumpsuit.

Remember what Tim Keller said? Our beliefs about the future shape the choices we make in the present. *The Wire* is one version of what happens when people believe the future is inescapably awful. When a story about this kind of future takes over even a small corner of a culture, countless lives are ravaged by the fallout. The fallout is succinctly articulated by a character named Slim Charles when he says, "Murder ain't no thing." Clearly, that's an awful story, and *The Wire* is an exposition of people who believe it. Absent a better story, is there any program or preventative measure that can transform *The Wire*—or the real world, for that matter—from tragedy to comedy?

Near the end of *The Shawshank Redemption*, Andy Dufresne writes a letter to his friend Red. "Remember, Red," Andy said, "hope is a good thing—maybe the best of things—and no good thing ever dies." Hope is the belief, however tenuous, that the story gets better. Andy Dufresne believed it, and *Shawshank* is the story of how he overcame years of atrocities and eventually gained his freedom. Omar, Stringer, Bodie, and Proposition Joe didn't believe the story got better, so *The Wire* is an account of them embracing the life-and-death stakes of the game.

> In understanding and being understood, we find ourselves with an intimate opportunity to tell a meaningful story about the hope we've found.

A number of stories are available in our culture. Some say money is hope. Some say sex and relationships are hope. Some say perception and reputation are hope. Some say power is hope. Some say nationalism and unencumbered liberty are hope. Some say there is no hope. When we look past culture to the individual people in our lives and communities, we're likely to see they're subscribed to one of these stories. In understanding what story (or stories) holds sway over a man's beliefs about himself and his future, we find ourselves closer to understanding the man. In understanding and being understood, we find ourselves with an intimate opportunity to tell a meaningful story about the hope we've found.

Remember, hope is a good thing.

CULTURE AND THE MAN IN THE DITCH

Perhaps I transitioned too abruptly in that last paragraph. Why look past culture to individuals? Aren't we supposed to be about the work of changing the world? Yes and no.

It seems right and good that we would echo our Father's love for the world as established in John 3:16. Yet, out of God's love for the world He took action to change the world. The thing is, He's God and we're not. Changing the world is a decidedly God-sized endeavor. And while 1 Corinthians 13 describes a grand vision of big love, the message seems to be directed at the *quality*, rather than *quantity*, of love. A set of commandments about love, found in Mark 12:29–31 and elsewhere, which we might take to be universal, instructs us to love the Lord with all we are and to love our neighbors as ourselves. The calling isn't to individually and specifically show love to each of the seven billion people on the planet, but rather to love people as we have opportunity.

> All you've been asked to do is be a witness, to tell your story in whatever time and place you find yourself.

Similarly, chapter 6 of this book makes a universal instruction out of the Acts 1:20 directive to be witnesses. Yes, enough witnesses may change the world, God willing, but we must not confuse the instruction with the result. I believe the distinction is crucial because our understanding inevitably shapes our expectations, attitudes, and methods. Those who believe their calling is to be a witness are grateful for an opportunity and a receptive ear. They're grateful for a conversation. They're grateful for a meal shared with a neighbor. However, those burdened with the pressure to change the world can't stop until they've ascended or manufactured a platform. See, the world's a big place, and changing it requires big influence, big messages, and big audiences. In fact, some culture writers (e.g., the aforementioned Hunter and Crouch) cast serious aspersions on the notion that we as individuals can change the world at all, regardless of our pure hearts, good intentions, or dogged determination.

I hope you get the opportunity to speak to our culture and change some fraction of the world if that's what God has for you. But I don't view that pursuit as a universal mandate for all who follow Christ. All you've been asked to do is be a witness, to tell your story in whatever time and place you find yourself. You're not responsible for leading an ideological conquest of the West. You're not obligated to transform yourself into a cultural icon so that you can present the gospel to your millions of fans.

Some people of faith do ascend to impressive platforms. They are politicians and athletes and artists who express their convictions in front of the masses. Justin Bieber, for instance, has the face of Jesus tattooed on his calf. So there's that. But I think it's fair to say The Biebs is not specifically emblematic of the lives we're meant to live as storytellers. That's not a knock on Mr. Bieber—it's just that we need not aspire to his level of global cachet in order to make a difference.

We're not called to change the world, nor do we have the ability to change people. We're just called to be witnesses. If enough people change so that the world changes, it'll simply be in response to the Story being told millions of times by millions of relatively anonymous storytellers. The Good Samaritan was not a doctor and wasn't responsible for healing the man in the ditch, and neither was he responsible for ending the world's violence or filling in the world's ditches. The Samaritan only had to dignify the man in the ditch as a human being made in the image of God and love him well—to Jesus, this was the story of a man who'd born witness to the eternal life in him by loving his neighbor.[5] The lives and stories of others make it clear they're in a ditch. They're wounded and isolated and ignored. Our role is to tell them the ever-hopeful Story into which they're invited.

"I'LL PROVIDE, YOU DISTRIBUTE."

In Mark 6, Jesus looks out at the crowd gathered to hear Him speak, and He sees how lost they are. Naturally, He has compassion on them. His disciples know the people will be hungry soon, so they want Jesus to send the crowd away to fend for themselves. Although the disciples' intentions were practical and somewhat benevolent, Jesus has a different idea—He wants His disciples to be a part of caring for the people He loves so much.

Just as in Acts 1, which we examined in chapter 4, the disciples look to Jesus to do something. "Send the people away so that they can go to the surrounding countryside and villages and buy themselves something to eat," the disciples said. But Jesus looked right back at them: *"You* give them something to eat."[6]

The disciples' response is understandably pragmatic even though Mark's gospel up to this point is the account of the disciples witnessing *and performing* miraculous events. "[Feeding the crowd] would take more than half a year's wages!" they exclaimed. Jesus simply asked them to take inventory of what they had: five loaves and two fish. In His power and provision, Jesus multiplied the food so there was more than enough to feed the hungry crowd. Still, the disciples had a job to do. "He gave [the loaves] to his disciples to distribute to the people."[7]

When you survey the stories at work in our culture, you might be troubled—Paul was distressed in Athens, after all. It's okay to conclude that most people in our world are like sheep without a shepherd—that was Jesus' feeling when He surveyed the crowd. But if our aim is to follow Christ, it's *not* okay to harbor any reaction other than compassion. We might be tempted to pray, "God, these people are hungry. Will You help them figure it out on their own?" If Mark 6 is any indication, we know what God's response will be. "You give them something to eat. I'll provide; you distribute."

Does our culture need a better story? There is no question. The sheep need a shepherd. What should we do about that? We should give them something to eat. We should be His witnesses. We should speak about what we've seen and heard. We should tell them a story.

When Jesus reinstates Peter in John 21, they have a conversation that goes like this:

> "Simon son of John, do you love me more than these?" Jesus asked.
>
> "Yes, Lord," he said. "You know that I love you."
>
> "Feed my lambs," Jesus responds. Then he asks again, "Simon son of John, do you love me?"
>
> "Yes, Lord, you know that I love you."
>
> "Take care of my sheep," Jesus responds. Then he asks a third time, "Simon son of John, do you love me?"
>
> "Lord, you know all things; you know that I love you," Peter insists.
>
> "Feed my sheep," Jesus says.[8]

Again, Jesus' heart for humanity is laid bare. And again, He enlists His disciples in the care of His loved ones. For storytellers who love Jesus, the call is strikingly simple: give the people something to eat. Give them a story of everlasting substance, the only story that can sate their hunger.

"MY NAME IS DULCINEA."

Man of La Mancha is a musical interpretation of Miguel de Cervantes's classic book *Don Quixote*. It's the story of a confused knight who mistakes a windmill for an enemy and a shabby inn for a castle. Don Quixote also mistakes Aldonza, a prostitute, for a proper lady named Dulcinea. Despite Aldonza's protests, Quixote can only see her as Dulcinea. Through word, deed, and of course, song, he tells her a story of what she could be—a story of beauty, honor, virtue, love, and glory.

Despite Aldonza's annoyance and outright resistance, the revelation of *Man of La Mancha* is the transformative power of a loving story. Aldonza can only see a future that mirrors her past and present—use and abuse, sin and shame. Quixote can only see Dulcinea, and thus can only treat Aldonza as such.

At the end of the story, Don Quixote dies and the woman he loves pauses to mourn him. When Quixote's sidekick Sancho calls her Aldonza, she declares, "My name is Dulcinea." How could she respond any other way? The story Don Quixote told to Aldonza about herself turned out to be the truth; his love and conviction made it so.[9] In the end, she couldn't resist.

In our interactions with others, we must be storytellers. That's not to say we should be delusional or easily confused as Don Quixote was, but neither should we be cynical. Rather, the story of the gospel is one of hope. To the woman caught in the act of adultery, Jesus said, "Neither do I condemn you. Go now and leave your life of sin."[10] To the Samaritan woman at the well, Jesus looked beyond the revolving door of relationships in her life, and instead offered a story in which she worshiped God in Spirit and truth, and in which she drank of the living water and never thirsted again.[11]

We all know Jesus predicted that Peter would deny Him three times the night He was betrayed. But just before that, in Luke 22,

Jesus looks further into Peter's story. He looks beyond the denial and imagines a mission of hope and redemption for Peter.

"Simon, Simon, Satan has asked to sift all of you as wheat. But I have prayed for you Simon, that your faith may not fail. *And when you have turned back,* strengthen your brothers" (vv. 31–32).

When Jesus was confronted with these people's past and present shortcomings, He didn't deny or ignore their weakness. He responded with compassion and offered them a better story.

POSSIBILITIES

Knowing our own story, an idea we explored in chapter 2, can tempt us toward solipsism or empathy. My hope is that you choose empathy—that knowing your story reminds you that everyone you meet has a story, too. After all, you're not the only person with a past, present, and future. You're not the only person who's chasing something. You're not the only person with scars. When it comes to others, I hope being a storyteller makes you curious, concerned, and compassionate.

So we have a choice to make regarding the story we'll tell about others. We can either imagine them fully alive as the people God made them to be or we can constrain them to the sum of their past and present successes and failures. My belief is that storytellers who are convinced of the message and activity of the gospel choose imagination. The gospel, as we've already said, is a story

> Thoreau said, "The question is not what you look at, but what you see."

about redemption, and it's this redemption we imagine when we invite others to both lose and find themselves in the story of God.

My daughter has a children's book in which the author describes a paintbrush, teeming with possibilities, as whispering, "Come and try me. There's a picture inside me." I love that the paintbrush beckons the child to see what is *hidden* or what *could be* rather than what is *apparent* or what *is*. If we've come this far, if we've accepted our callings as storytellers, then we have to begin seeing people like they're whispering paintbrushes. If they're human, there's a story inside them whether they know it or not. As Thoreau said, "The question is not what you look at, but what you see."[12]

Jesus looked at water and saw wine. He looked at the lame and saw dancers. Jesus looked at the cross and saw victory. He looked at the tomb and saw it empty. Jesus looked at a disparate collection of rugged Jewish men and saw His first witnesses. He looked at a world ravaged by rebellion and saw it made new.

Through grace Jesus gives us new life, new words, and a new story. He also gives us new eyes through which to see. In ourselves we see storytellers, called to bear witness to our rescue by God and our relationship with God. In others we see fellow storytellers and those not yet awakened to the story of faith, hope, and love.

WADE IN

Yes, the waters of culture are polluted. But Jesus wades in. Yes, the lives of others can be complicated and messy. But Jesus gets His hands dirty. Do you understand your calling as a Christian any differently? I hope not.

See, we can't be witnesses from the sidelines. We can't tell a story from the other side of the street. We can't abstain from culture and still hope to affect it. We must listen to and take part in the stories of others. Along the way, you'll hear hundreds of stories that make something of the world, but none will be as wide and long and high and deep as the love of Christ expressed in the Story.

So we must tell stories of our own. We must engage and we must imagine and we must give them something to eat . . . because that is what storytellers do.

the storyteller, church, and community

"We must engage and we must imagine and we must give them something . . . because that is what storytellers do."

COMMUNITY DOESN'T COME EASY TO us in the 21st century—too many forces tempt us toward pride, self-centeredness, and isolation. A few in particular should suffice to make the point.

ADS, AUTOS, ON, AND IN

Externally, these forces take a few forms: advertising that teaches us to focus on satisfying our emotional and material needs; automobiles that invite us to spread the various facets of our lives (friends, family, work, school, church) across a wide geographic area; and mobile electronic devices that are always on, always connected, and always alerting us to inanity we consider information.

Internally, the temptation toward pride, self-centeredness, and isolation need not take a form in order to be persuasive—this temptation resides at the very core of our fractured selves, constrained only by a thin crust of civility, compelling us to grab for control of our circumstances at every turn. This impulse is the reason many romantic, platonic, professional, and spiritual relationships devolve into mistrust and power struggles before ultimately dissolving. There's just something about me that defaults to putting me first, and I suspect you're wired the same way. This is why I don't trust you, and not trusting you adds more fuel to my impulse to protect and serve myself.

But of course, despite my impulses to the contrary, a life lived in service to self isn't much of a story.

WE, NOT ME

As dutiful products of Enlightenment thinking, we tend to think of ourselves as individuals who think, feel, and choose for ourselves. This tendency is understandable, but it's also inaccurate. Scientists who used to think of an individual brain as independent and sovereign within its skull now understand that human beings are inextricably connected on a neurological level:

> The problem with this "single skull" perspective—where we consider each individual brain as a lone organ isolated in a single skull—is that it neglects the truth that scientists have come to understand over the last few decades: that the brain is a social organ, made to be in relationship. It's hardwired to take in signals from the social environment, which in turn influence a person's inner world. In other words, what happens *between* brains has a great deal to do with what happens *within* each individual brain. Self and community are fundamentally interrelated, since every brain is continually constructed by its interactions with others. Even more, studies of happiness and wisdom reveal that a key factor in well-being is devoting one's attention and passions to the benefit of theirs instead of just focusing on the individual, separate concerns of a private self. The "me" discovers meaning and happiness by joining and belonging to a "we."[1]

The implication of these findings is that humans aren't just superficially affected by others—we're *shaped* by others. This dynamic, this susceptibility to interaction, this ingrained bent toward community suggests we were made to be together. If this is true—if we cannot escape the influence, for better or worse, of those around us—it stands to reason that a particular community might have a particular effect upon a person. In fact, great stories teach us that our individual lives are richer and more meaningful when we pursue objectives and persist through conflict while in community. Our characters are refined, our pursuits are vetted, and our burdens are shared in community, and we find this truth present in the narratives that capture our hearts and minds.

If you consider your favorite stories from film, literature, or history, you'll find they all feature more than one character. Even when one character is more prominent than the rest, the best stories use a community of supporting characters to move the protagonist toward wisdom, courage, and sacrifice. Many of the stories that speak to me pit a community against what appears to be insurmountable conflict, from *The Lord of the Rings* trilogy to *The Mission* to *Lost* to *Firefly*. It's in these stories, in which people and circumstances construct a redemptive community using their individual gifts and histories, that I'm reminded of the truth God spoke shortly after the dawn of humanity: "It is not good for the man to be alone."[2] We're all given a self-container we call a body, and yet story reminds us we were never meant to be self-contained. On the contrary, we're most alive in healthy relationships. The same story that beckons us to be fully alive also beckons us to relationship and community.

The very idea of a storyteller is intrinsically relational. The title of this book—*Tell Me a Story*—was chosen because it implies a conversation between two or more people, speaking and listening, sharing and connecting. The isolated storyteller is as much a walking contradiction as a self-professed football player who limits himself to throwing the ball through a tire swing. He's not a football player until he gets in the game with twenty-one other players. And just as no football players or great stories exist in isolation, neither do any great storytellers.

One of my favorite films, *Cast Away*, depicts its protagonist in extended isolation, but the film never advocates for extended isolation. Instead, the story's most powerful moments occur when Chuck Noland is ripped away from his community and when he risks his life to return home to his community. We simply don't find any great stories about disconnected individuals who pursue an honorable objective and persevere through conflict in isolation. Neither do we find any records of saints who were both perfectly isolated *and* faithful witnesses.

THE UNENDING STORY

If you think about creation and life in the garden as depicted in Genesis 1 and 2, it might be most difficult to get your head around a world in which humanity was not yet stained by sin. The next most difficult idea to imagine might be that at first there was only one human, Adam. When we combine these two aspects of the story, we find that while God deemed Adam good, God also deemed Adam's aloneness not good. God then took it upon Himself to make for Adam a proper companion.

In *Searching for God Knows What*, Donald Miller explores the implication that Adam was both good and incomplete. In other words, Adam's untarnished integrity did not make him self-sufficient. In Adam God observed some dynamic of loneliness or need that moved Him to make Eve. "It is a striking thought to realize that, in paradise, a human is incomplete without a host of other people," he writes. "We are relational indeed."[3]

Despite our relational wiring, every human relationship has the potential to splinter and cite "irreconcilable differences" because wherever humans are involved, divergent interests follow. But in order to turn our focus from ourselves and come together, we need a bigger story than the kind of collaboration a child might propose: "On the count of three, you give me what I want."

A bigger story is the dynamic at work in the church, of course, but it's not an exclusively ecclesiastic principle—leaders everywhere employ this approach. Vince Lombardi convinced his players to buy into a bigger story. Generals, politicians, and CEOs do it, too. The difference is that the bigger story of the church is eternal rather than ephemeral.

> The stories of trophies won, markets conquered, armies defeated, and days seized eventually fade away, but the story of the church in Christ persists.

The stories of trophies won, markets conquered, armies defeated, and days seized eventually fade away—even *The NeverEnding Story* ended—but the story of the church in Christ persists.

As I've pondered the gospel and the hyper-accelerated, ever-changing nature of our culture, I've come to believe the church has unique and powerful words at its disposal. Stories abound in our world, but it is the church that coalesces and makes this monumental claim about its story: *everlasting*. The people of God serve one another well when we stake our fellowship to the kingdom without end. To the extent that we can give voice to this truth in our worship services, from readings (e.g., Psalm 136, Psalm 145) to music (e.g., "Amazing Grace," "From the Inside Out") to teaching, we anchor ourselves to that which both pervades and transcends our day and age.

When we cover one another in God's unending story—in which we have a place—we more readily heed His instruction to be not afraid, we more readily give of ourselves with reckless generosity, and we more readily reject distractions such as culture wars and the American Dream. The everlasting story binds us in relationship with Him and others, for His glory and our good.

CHURCH, STORY, AND PURPOSE

We see story as a common theme in N. T. Wright's definition of the church as a community with an identity informed by its past, present, and future: "The church is the single, multiethnic family promised by the creator God to Abraham. It was brought into being through Israel's Messiah, Jesus; it was energized by God's Spirit; and it was called to bring the transformative news of God's rescuing justice to the whole creation."[4]

Wright also characterizes the purpose of the church as found in the New Testament this way: "that through the church God will announce to the wider world that he is indeed its wise, loving, and just creator; that through Jesus he has defeated the powers that corrupt and enslave it; and that by his Spirit he is at work to heal and renew it."[5]

> Though this community is composed of unique individuals, we're bound together by the gospel story and its redemptive work in our lives.

We might summarize Wright's words by saying the church exists to bear witness to the person of God as revealed in His story—what He has done, what He is doing, and what He will do. This is the mission for which we have been equipped and sent. This is the life for which we have been rescued from our graves. This is the tribe into which we've been reborn.

"The church is first and foremost a *community,*" Wright says, "a collection of people who belong to one another because they belong to God, the God we know in and through Jesus."[6] This community exists primarily, he writes, "to worship God and to work for his kingdom in the world," but also "for a third purpose which serves the other two: to encourage one another, to build one another up in faith, to pray with and for one another, to learn from one another and teach one another, and to set one another examples to follow, challenges to take up, and urgent tasks to perform."[7]

Though this community is composed of unique individuals, we're bound together by the gospel story and its redemptive work in our lives. And while much of the broader Christian conversation in the West seems to focus on our differences, Jesus made a point to pray publicly to the Father that all who believe would be one, that we would be "brought to complete unity," because such unity is a witness to both the divinity of Christ and the generous love of God.[8] In the church, the story of God fosters community, and community bears witness to the story.

A COMMUNAL PRACTICE

Communion, or the Eucharist, is an inherently communal practice, at the center of which Jesus placed both His story and our mandate to be storytellers. First, there's His story: He explains the bread and the cup are His body and blood given for us. Then there's the storyteller imperative: we are to partake of the bread and the cup in *remembrance*[9] of Him. To remember is to tell, either out loud or in the quiet of our own hearts, the story that brings us to the table in the first place. Bullet points and clever Christian T-shirts have no place here—only remembrance of the person and journey of our Lord will suffice.

As it relates to community, it's to our benefit to remember that on the night He was betrayed, Jesus didn't hand each of the disciples his own loaf of bread. Rather, He broke the bread and distributed the pieces, symbolizing both His body and the community for which it was broken. He didn't meet with His disciples one-on-one to share the holy moment with them as individuals; He chose His moment when they were all gathered around a table. It's fitting that Jesus hosted this communal meal on His way to the cross—He was headed there to secure for Himself a people by trading one body for another.

We are His witnesses, and we live out this identity in both community and communion. "For whenever you eat this bread and drink this cup," Paul wrote to the believers at Corinth, "you proclaim the Lord's death until he comes."[10]

COMMUNITY IN PRACTICE

In the introduction I mentioned the community that formed around our adoption process and its ups and downs. The adoption started as my family's story—our choice, our burdens, our emotions—but I don't know if Annie and I could have done it alone. A community can delve deeper into a story than an individual can because where one person might lose the will or the way, a community can find the resources to keep going. In our story, the people who joined us in our adoption journey helped us in

> Your story is meant to be enjoined with other life stories in the telling of God's story.

ways we often struggled to help ourselves: prayer, comfort, company, counsel, encouragement, finances, and logistics. In hindsight, having experienced this holy synergy, I was both grateful for the people God used in our story and sad that some families, through choice or circumstance, end up walking that road alone.

It was through this experience I realized I hadn't understood much about the church before. Both the story and the community were exponentially more active and immersive than I previously imagined. I'd settled—and I expect I'm not alone in this—for mere attendance, mere assembly, when our calling is something more like fellowship, a dynamic participation in the communion of the saints and ministry in the name of Jesus.

One shortcoming of the popular napkin-scribble gospel illustration depicting a person on one side and God on the other side of a chasm created by sin is that Christ's cross-bridge simply creates "a way for you to get to God," but nothing more. Yes, Christ has helped you mediate the chasm created by your sin, and yes, you depart to be with the Lord when you die, but something's missing. Lost in the flat, black-and-white napkin scribbles is the rich color and depth of life with Christ in community.

I suppose you may now be perturbed. We've come all this way together, and then at this point I surprise you by taking a shot at what might be the most popular gospel illustration of our day. I'm sorry about that, and I hope my meaning isn't lost. My argument is simply this: Your life story was never meant to stand alone. Your story is meant to be enjoined with other life stories in the telling of God's story. I've told you several times you're called to be a witness, but perhaps that's too singular. *We* are called to be witness*es*.

The depth of our calling is designed to be plumbed in community. As we are transformed by God's story, we gather around it, and as we gather around God's story, we are transformed by it. We celebrate the story and we mine it and we wrestle it. We tell it to each other and to our children and to our neighbors. The effect of this story community is a kind of slow, covert magic—a few years go by and you realize you can't truly tell your own story without mentioning God and Jesus and *all those people* who walked with you. You realize that word—*enjoined*—has just happened somewhere along the way. You're in community.

THE CHURCH MUST . . .

The shared conviction that a church is meant to be a story-telling collective that bears witness to the gospel *and* bears one another's burdens changes the inward workings and outward expressions of a local body of believers. In the church there exists something that cannot exist in an empire, a republic, a federation, a state, a city, a neighborhood, even a social club: community rooted in the story of God and indwelled by His Spirit. As a result, I believe there are a few things the church must do.

I believe we must be careful observers and communicators of God's story as found in Scripture, in our lives, and as it continues to unfold. We must gather in fellowship around the story of God, celebrate it, and worship our Creator and Redeemer. Morality is not enough to bind us. Obligation is not enough to move us. We have to be caught up in a common story.

We must invite people into the story, to believe in the events and the hope of the gospel. We must challenge ourselves and our neighbors to follow Christ as He leads us to be better characters in better stories. We must awaken to the ongoing story of God as expressed in the ministry and mission of the body of Christ. We must likewise call others to come awake. We must teach people to be storytellers, to speak meaning and hope amid chaos. We must be attentive storytellers who listen with empathy to the stories of others because human beings merit human connections.

The church must imbue people with the conviction that God is the Creator and Lover of our souls; that Jesus lived, died, and rose to free us from sin into relationship with Him; that His Spirit guides us, comforts us, and empowers us to live stories permeated by love, joy, peace, patience, kindness, goodness, faithfulness, gentleness, and self-control. Likewise, our stories must be characterized by the holy union of orthodoxy (right belief) and orthopraxy (right action), and in fact all great stories reflect this union in some way or another. Our faith and our stories must embody both communion and commission.

We must not squander our opportunity to experience our individual stories in the context of community. Let us discover and pursue our objectives and callings in community. Let us explore and express our purpose in community. Let us engage and endure conflict in community. Let us grieve and cheer and strain and stride together, step after step, toward denouements big and small. Let us pray and share and partner.

> We must likewise call others to come awake. We must teach people to be storytellers, to speak meaning and hope amid chaos.

When we gather, we must teach in such a way as to connect specific Scripture passages to the overarching story of God from which they originate. We must sing in such a way as to give words to God's greatness, character, and activity, as well as our response. We must pray in such a way as to remember God's faithfulness in the past, express our gratitude in the present, and anticipate His presence and provision in the future. We must be a *people,* not just a place, where Psalm 105 finds true expression:

> Give praise to the Lord, proclaim his name;
> make known among the nations what he has done.
> Sing to him, sing praise to him;
> tell of all his wonderful acts.
> Glory in his holy name;
> let the hearts of those who seek the Lord rejoice.
> Look to the Lord and his strength;
> seek his face always.
> Remember the wonders he has done,
> his miracles, and the judgments he pronounced,

you his servants, the descendants of Abraham,
his chosen ones, the children of Jacob. (vv. 1–6)

This is a community that cannot separate itself from the story of God as it has been revealed in their midst. They worship, they remember, they bear witness.

When a community decides to tell a great story, amazing things happen. But communities and great stories don't happen by accident—they're the result of intention. May we be the kind of people who keep in step with the Spirit as we're guided into deep fellowship and deep stories.

We must be His witnesses, but we must not attempt to establish our witness through belligerent street-corner prattling, vacuous billboards and bumper stickers, promotional gimmickry, or futile political machinations. The body of Christ need not employ the tactics of a carnival barker, ambulance chaser, or snake oil salesman—not when our bodies are "members of Christ himself."[11]

Rather we must aspire to the kind of community that is by very nature a witness. Hauerwas and Willimon call this community *the confessing church*, a body which "seeks the visible church, a place, clearly visible to the world, in which people are faithful to their promises, love their enemies, tell the truth, honor the poor, suffer for righteousness, and thereby testify to the amazing community-creating power of God. . . . This church knows that its most credible form of witness (and the most 'effective' thing it can do for the world) is the actual creation of a living, breathing, visible community of faith."[12]

THE PEOPLE OF THE RESURRECTION

I was at a conference four years ago when I heard a simple but profound articulation of this vision for a community that exudes—rather than screams—witness. An audience member asked film producer and believer Todd Komarnicki *(Elf, Meet Dave)* what manner of strategy Christians should employ in order to infiltrate and impact Hollywood. Was it networking or interning? Was it screenwriting or producing? Was it acting or directing? What were the beats needed to change the culture?

Komarnicki's answer favored presence to process: "We are the people of the resurrection," he declared. "Let's be that."

I've thought about those words often since I first heard them, and while they remain brief, for me their meaning continues to deepen. *We are the people of the resurrection.* The apostle Paul even connected our identity in the resurrection with our identity as witnesses:

> We always carry around in our body the death of Jesus, so that the life of Jesus may also be revealed in our body. For we who are alive are always being given over to death for Jesus' sake, so that his life may also be revealed in our mortal body. So then, death is at work in us, but life is at work in you.
>
> It is written: "I believed; therefore I have spoken." Since we have that same spirit of faith, we also believe and therefore speak, because we know that the one who raised the Lord Jesus from the dead will also raise us with Jesus and present us with you to himself.[13]

The story of Jesus—His life, death, and resurrection—is echoed in our own stories. We believe it, we speak it, and one day we will rise. We are the people of the resurrection—that's our story. Let's be that.

metamorphosis

We may consider great storytellers to be those who have mastered the elements and tools—structure, character, dialogue, prose, oratory, suspense, and so on—but we mustn't forget their dedication to seeing. A storyteller sees the world as it is and as it could be. A storyteller sees the difference between what he was and what he is becoming. A storyteller sees others as people God carefully created and intensely loves. A storyteller sees God at work. And once we begin to see, the elements and tools of story take on new potency in our hands.

My hope is that this book has, in some small way, helped you see that you were created to live and tell great stories in the service of His kingdom. Being storytellers in the kingdom of God does not mean we know the future or believe we can write it to our whims. Rather, being storytellers in the kingdom of God means as we live in fellowship with Christ and His church, we remember on purpose, we bear witness on purpose, and we press forward on purpose. We're mindful of the story we find ourselves in, and we tell it with conviction. We can't keep quiet.

As you go on your way, you will find that telling a story of both tragedy and hope—that things are broken, and yet there is One whose love mends—will make you a rare bird indeed, but that is the truth of God's story. You're not responsible for justifying, defending, amending, or force-feeding this story—just bear witness to it in word and deed. In so doing, your narrative will confront people with the possibility of redemption and transformation in Christ.

Back in chapter 1 we saw Robert McKee's insistence that a story must deliver absolute and irreversible change to its main character(s), and this idea is as true for Job as it is for Jason Bourne. Tolkien was showing us transformation when he slowly matured those four meek hobbits into heroes. In the Bible, Peter goes from denying Jesus the night He was betrayed to preaching in front of thousands on the day of Pentecost. This is the kind of transformation that happens when a hapless young fisherman is beckoned into a great story by a rabbi who also happens to be Messiah because God is always about this business of calling ordinary people into extraordinary stories.

And as for us, well, we're never the same again.

notes

PREFACE
things fall apart

1. Lauren F. Winner, *Still: Notes on a Mid-Faith Crisis* (New York: HarperCollins, 2012), Kindle edition.

CHAPTER ONE
story: a new way to see

1. 1 Peter 5:7.

2. Genesis 32:25–31 MSG.

3. Genesis 33:11 MSG.

4. Robert McKee, *Story* (New York: HarperCollins, 1997), 41.

5. Donald Miller, *A Million Miles in a Thousand Years: What I Learned While Editing My Life* (Nashville: Thomas Nelson, 2009), 48.

6. "Kurt Vonnegut at the Blackboard," accessed February 18, 2012, http://www.laphams quarterly.org/voices-in-time/kurt-vonnegut-at-the-blackboard.php?page=all.

7. James Scott Bell, *Write Great Fiction—Plot & Structure* (Cincinnati: F+W Publications, 2004), 11.

8. Frederick Buechner, *Telling the Truth: The Gospel as Tragedy, Comedy, and Fairy Tale* (New York: HarperCollins, 1977), 90.

9. Henri Nouwen, *The Wounded Healer* (New York: Doubleday, 1972), 92.

10. "Filmmakers' Conversation – Episode 3." RelevantMagazine.com, accessed February 21, 2012, http://www.relevantmagazine.com/blue-jazz/behind-scenes/filmmakers-conversation-episode-3.

11. William Shakespeare, *Henry IV, Part 1*, III.1.1601.

CHAPTER TWO
character: ourselves, close-up

1. Daniel Siegel and Tina Payne Bryson, *The Whole-Brain Child* (New York: Delacorte Press, 2011), 29.

2. Alan D. Wolfelt, "Companioning the Bereaved: An Introduction," accessed February 24, 2012, http://www.texashealth.org/body.cfm?id=3632.

3. Lauren Winner, *Still: Notes on a Mid-Faith Crisis* (New York: HarperCollins, 2012), 55–56.

4. Margaret C. Harrell and Nancy Berglass, "Losing the Battle: The Challenge of Military Suicide," accessed February 24, 2012, http://www.cnas.org/files/documents/publications/CNAS_LosingTheBattle_HarrellBerglass_0.pdf.

5. Anna Mulrine, "Army report: Suicide rate sets record; some alcohol abuse up 54 percent," *The Christian Science Monitor*, accessed February 26, 2012, http://www.csmonitor.com/USA/Military/2012/0120/Army-report-Suicide-rate-sets-record-some-alcohol-abuse-up-54-percent.

6. "Should I Not Love That Great City?" narrated by Timothy Keller, Timothy Keller Podcast, February 10, 2010, http://sermons2.redeemer.com/sites/sermons2.redeemer.com/files/RSS_Feeds/Timothy_Keller_Podcasts.xml.

7. Siegel and Bryson, *The Whole-Brain Child*, 5.

8. Ibid.

9. Ian Morgan Cron, *Jesus, My Father, the CIA, and Me: A Memoir of Sorts* (Nashville: Thomas Nelson, 2011), 235.

CHAPTER THREE
narrator: God

1. Tim the Enchanter is the frightening character in *Monty Python and the Holy Grail* who shows off his ability to blow things up.

2. Sally Lloyd-Jones, "Teach Children the Bible Is Not About Them," The Gospel Coalition, accessed May 18, 2012, http://thegospelcoalition.org/blogs/tgc/2012/02/21/teach-children-the-bible-is-not-about-them/.

3. "King and a Kingdom," narrated by Barry Jones, Irving Bible Church, April 15, 2012, http://www.irvingbible.org/media/view/message/king-and-a-kingdom/.

4. Skye Jethani, *With: Reimagining the Way You Relate to God* (Nashville: Thomas Nelson, 2011), 61.

5. Ibid.

6. Gladding has cleverly named these installments Creation, Catastrophe, Covenant, Community, Conquest, Crown, Conceit, Christ, Cross, Church, and Consummation.

7. Sean Gladding, *The Story of God, the Story of Us* (Downers Grove, IL: InterVarsity Press, 2010), 21.

8. Scot McKnight, *The King Jesus Gospel: The Original Good News Revisited* (Grand Rapids: Zondervan, 2011), 36.

9. Ibid.

10. Cited in Lauren Winner, *Still: Notes on a Mid-Faith Crisis* (New York: HarperCollins, 2012), 193.

CHAPTER FOUR
objective: make something

1. Mako Fujimura, "What Do You Want To Make Today?" YouTube, accessed May 28, 2012, http://www.youtube.com/watch?v=euBe4PxKz_M&..

2. Frank Capra, *The Name Above the Title: An Autobiography* (Cambridge, MA, Da Capo Press, 1997), xxi.

3. James Davison Hunter, *To Change the World: The Irony, Tragedy, and Possibility of Christianity in the Late Modern World* (New York: Oxford University Press, 2010), 3.

4. G.K. Chesterton, *Orthodoxy* (Chicago: Moody, 2009 edition), 33.

5. Bob Goff, *Love Does: Discover a Secretly Incredible Life in an Ordinary World* (Nashville: Thomas Nelson, 2012), 181.

6. Genesis 2:16–17.

7. Erwin McManus, phone conversation with author, March 28, 2012.

8. This quote is attributed to various people, and yet there is no clear consensus on its true origin. Go figure.

9. "Basava," Wikipedia.org, accessed June 19, 2012, http://en.wikipedia.org/wiki/Basava.

10. Colossians 3:23–24.

CHAPTER FIVE
conflict: all is lost

1. John 16:33.

2. Michael Monroe, "Being Thankful for the Broken Things," accessed June 25, 2012, http://tapestryministry.org/being-thankful-for-the-broken-things.

3. James Scott Bell, *Write Great Fiction—Plot & Structure* (Cincinnati: F+W Publications, 2004), 15.

4. Kurt Vonnegut, *Bagombo Snuff Box: Uncollected Short Fiction* (New York: G.P. Putnam's Sons, 1999), 10.

5. "002—Echoes of Eden," narrated by Ian Cron and Andy Traub, *Learning To See with Ian Morgan Cron,* accessed March 30, 2012, http://www.iancron.com/2012/03/29/002/.

6. Blaine Hogan, "Breathing Through Your Work," accessed March 29, 2012, http://www.blainehogan.com/post/20065012683/breathing-through-your-work.

7. Rob Bell, *Drops Like Stars* (Grand Rapids: Zondervan, 2009), 24.

8. Miroslav Volf, *The End of Memory: Remembering Rightly in a Violent World* (Grand Rapids: Eerdmans, 2006), 77.

9. Ibid., 93.

10. Ibid., 100.

11. Genesis 50:19–20.

12. J.R.R. Tolkein, *The Silmarillion,* Second Edition (Boston: Houghton Mifflin Harcourt, 1977), accessed July 6, 2012, http://books.google.com/books?id=4OfWWfRDAXcC.

13. Henri Nouwen, *The Wounded Healer* (New York: Doubleday, 1972), 82–83.

14. 1 Corinthians 1:27 NIV, 1984.

15. John 20:27.

purpose: beyond the macguffin

1. Brian Hiatt, "'Darkness' Revisited," *Rolling Stone,* November 25, 2010, 63.

2. Adam Pasick, "The Risks of Bearing Witness: Discussing Marie Colvin's Legacy," *New York Magazine,* accessed February 23, 2012, http://nymag.com/daily/intel/2012/02/risks-of-bearing-witness-marie-colvins-legacy.html.

3. Frederick Buechner, *Telling the Truth: The Gospel as Tragedy, Comedy, and Fairy Tale* (New York: HarperCollins, 1977), 16–17.

the storyteller, culture, and people

1. James Davison Hunter, *To Change the World: The Irony, Tragedy, and Possibility of Christianity in the Late Modern World* (New York: Oxford University Press, 2010), 32.

2. Andy Crouch, *Culture Making: Recovering Our Creative Calling* (Downers Grove, IL: InterVarsity Press, 2008), 23.

3. Hunter, *To Change the World,* 33.

4. Mark 7:20–23.

5. See Luke 10:29–37.

6. Mark 6:36–37.

7. Mark 6:41.

8. See John 21:15–17.

9. It was my pastor, Andy McQuitty, who introduced me to the redemptive story of Don Quixote and Aldonza in a sermon.

10. John 8:11.

11. John 4:10–24.

12. Henry David Thoreau, *The Writings of Henry David Thoreau* (Boston: Houghton Mifflin Co., 1906), http://www.walden.org/Library/The_Writings_of_Henry_David_Thoreau:_The_Digital_Collection/The_Writings_of_Henry_David_Thoreau_(1906).

CHAPTER EIGHT
the storyteller, church, and community

1. Daniel Siegel and Tina Payne Bryson, *The Whole-Brain Child* (New York: Delacorte Press, 2011), 122.

2. Genesis 2:18.

3. Donald Miller, *Searching for God Knows What* (Nashville: Thomas Nelson, 2004), 67.

4. N. T. Wright, *Simply Christian: Why Christianity Makes Sense* (New York: HarperCollins, 2006), 200.

5. Ibid., 204.

6. Ibid., 210.

7. Ibid., 211.

8. John 17:20–23.

9. Luke 22:19.

10. 1 Corinthians 11:26.

11. 1 Corinthians 6:15.

12. Stanley Hauerwas and William Willimon, *Resident Aliens: Life in the Christian Colony* (Nashville: Abingdon Press, 2008), 46–47.

13. 2 Corinthians 4:10–14.

acknowledgments

THERE ARE A NUMBER OF people who contributed to this book, both before and during its creation, and I'd be a fool not to acknowledge as many of them as I can.

First, I owe a debt of gratitude to the entire team at Moody Publishers for their encouragement and expertise, including Randall Payleitner, Pam Pugh, Natalie Mills, and so many others.

I must also thank a roster of good friends who, through their participation in various conversations and experiences, are collectively on the hook for shaping the way I think about the world. This list includes, but is not limited to, Brent Ashby, Gary Cottrell, John Dyer, Bryan Eck, Tim Entzminger, Jason Mitchell, Michael Monroe, Stephen Presley, Stephen Proctor, Matthew Slay, Rhett Smith, and Anthony Violi. There's also the leadership of Irving Bible Church, a community that has ministered to my family in immeasurable ways.

I have to thank my friends and colleagues at RT Creative Group, led by Rob Thomas and Jeff Parker, with whom I've had the pleasure of creating new resources for the church over the course of eight years.

And finally, I have to thank my wife, Annie. This book wouldn't exist without her patience, grace, and input. Writers have a tendency to get caught up in urgency, anxiety, and minutiae, and so many of us need someone who is grounded enough to talk us down from the rickety scaffolding of our current project. My wife is this source of perspective for me, and I can't imagine how I would've completed this work without her.

LIFE AFTER ART

978-0-8024-0739-9

We long to create without judgment from ourselves or others. We want the freedom to fail as we take risks. We want to remember not just what we created as children—paintings, clay pots, stories, songs, games—but how we created with such freedom.

In *Life After Art*, art teacher Matt Appling reminds us of the lessons we've forgotten since leaving the art room. He walks us through the steps in recapturing those lessons and points us back to the productive, contented, joy-filled lives that God created us to live.

moody
collective

Moody Collective brings words of life to a generation seeking deeper faith. We are a part of Moody Publishers, representing this next generation of followers of Christ through books, blogs, essays, and more.

We seek to know, love, and serve the millennial generation with grace and humility. Each of our books is intended to challenge and encourage our readers as they pursue God. To learn more, visit our website, www.moodycollective.com.

www.MoodyPublishers.com